I Give You My WORD

Sharing the Language of Life

C. WELTON GADDY
President of The Interfaith Alliance
Foreword by WALTER CRONKITE

ISBN: 1-932407-15-4

Library of Congress Cataloging-in-Publication Data Available

Design: Kerry DeAngelis, KL Design

New Millennium Press
301 North Canon Drive
Suite 214
Beverly Hills, CA 90210
www.newmillenniumpress.com

10 9 8 7 6 5 4 3 2 1

FOREWORD

I am happy to have the opportunity to share, and to welcome readers to, my friend Welton Gaddy's remarkable new book. *I Give You My Word: The Language of Life* celebrates the richness of diversity. Welton has asked many of his friends from around the world for the gift of One Word. He has heard back from many people, from all walks of life...some more renowned than others. Most of these words are in English. A few are not. Some are more obvious than others. Some are silly. Some are profound. This cornucopia of words and phrases is a personal gift to each and every one of us...the gift of meaning. These words will provoke. They'll make us think, they'll make us laugh, they'll cause us to reflect and ponder and they'll encourage us to share. What word would you choose? Why? Spread the wealth and share this gift with your friends and family.

Each word is the foundation of a thought or of a sentence, but each in its simplest form has a beauty all its own. It's that beauty that I celebrate and I invite you to join me.

In addition to my word gift to Welton that appears later in the volume, here are three more of my own contributions to *I Give You My Word,* and I apologize for not being able to choose just one.

COURAGE. In a difficult and tumultuous time, C. Welton Gaddy possesses the special courage to lead, and to share with us this unique project that gives new meaning to the language of life.

GRATITUDE. It's with immense gratitude that I thank Welton for gathering a collection of words that will allow our spirits to soar; a collection that will inspire thought and that begs to be shared; a collection that's offered in the spirit of good; and provides bright hopes. And last but certainly not least...

FREEDOM. In times of both war and peace it is necessary, even crucial, to never lose sight of what words mean, and the true gift that they bestow on us. Freedom to give voice to ALL points of view and ALL our myriad religions, philosophies, lifestyles, and directions has never been more important—offering us all amazing opportunity in the true sense of a global community.

—WALTER CRONKITE

INTRODUCTION

A PASSION FOR WORDS

"And now we come to the magic of words."
—EMMA JUNG

"What so wild as words are?"
—ROBERT BROWNING

To my great embarrassment, I cannot remember details of the experience that inspired this book. Many years ago, easily twenty or more, I read an account of a man's prized visit with a famous author; Hemingway, I think. After an extended time of conversation, the visitor made a strange request of the noted writer. Desiring a tangible remembrance of their time together, the visitor asked the author for the gift of a word—one word, one of the author's favorite words.

Though the specifics of that story left me long ago, the intriguing idea of the gift of a word lingered across the years. As words became increasingly important to me, an interest in knowing other people's favorite words developed from a fascination into a passion.

Obvious value endows a word shared by a merchant of words such as a best-selling author, a journalist, a religious leader, a public speaker, or a commentator in the electronic media. In reality, though, any individual's gift of a favored word—every individual's gift of a favored word—is a personal offering of no little significance.

Learning of a dramatic event during our nation's military involvement in the Korean conflict further heightened my interest in and enflamed my enthusiasm for word gifts. Here is the story. Enemy forces had brought a captured United States general before a firing squad. Just prior to issuing the command that would cost the American officer his life, the leader of the would-be executioners asked the general if he wished to speak or write any final words. *What would I do in such a situation?* I thought as I read an account of this emotion-laced moment. *With only a few breaths of life remaining, what words would I speak or write?* The general requested that a note be sent to his only son. The note read, "Tell Bill the word is 'integrity.'"

What an incredibly valuable gift! And the gift was a word.

I wanted to be the recipient of word gifts from people whom I likely never would know in any other way. After all, the gift of a personal word represents the sharing of a part of one's self. "For words, like Nature, half reveal and half conceal the Soul within," Tennyson wrote. People who allow others to know their favorite words provide a glimpse into their character, values, priorities, thoughts, hopes, and interests. A word shared between two or more people becomes a window through which those persons look at each other, maybe through which they peer into each other's minds or souls or both.

I resolved to find out if people—people whom I did not know and probably would never meet—would share a word with me.

WHAT'S IN A WORD?

"'When I use a word,' Humpty Dumpty said ... 'It means just what I choose it to mean— neither more or less.'"
—LEWIS CARROLL

"How long a time lies in one little word!"
—WILLIAM SHAKESPEARE

Mark Twain once observed that the difference between the right word and an almost-right word is the difference between lightning and a lightning bug. Contrary opinions about words, like that parroted in the old cliché "Words are cheap," display a serious lack of good judgment about the significance of words. True, words can be used cheaply—miserly, sloppily, manipulatively, deceptively, abusively. Some people prostitute words. Others ruthlessly rape them. Even then, though, the words themselves retain value. The worth of a word defies an exact estimate.

Words pack power, carry clout. A single word can create or destroy, sting or soothe, heal or injure, rip or patch, encourage or dishearten, entice or repel, entertain or frighten, help or hurt, unite or divide, cleanse or dirty, excite or depress, grace or judge, eroticize or desensitize, whip or massage, validate or void, lacerate or heal, inspire or deflate, instruct or confuse, separate or reconcile. Words wield inestimable strength and exercise immeasurable influence.

Words take on recognizable characters, each different from another. A word can be an upper or a downer, a zinger or a fizzle, a scream or a whimper, a hammer or a feather, a drum roll or a bugle blast, a hawk or a dove, a prayer or a protest, a blessing or a curse. Similarly, a word can be hot or cold, inclusive or exclusive, welcome or intrusive, poetic or pedestrian, visionary or moribund.

Actually, the method, mood, or tone involved in the delivery of a word often distinguishes the particular character of that word. David Garrick observed that George Whitefield, the noted nineteenth-century British evangelist, could make people either laugh or cry by the way he pronounced the word "Mesopotamia." A word can rise or droop, dance or plod, bloom or wilt, bounce or splatter, laugh or weep, explode or whimper, meander or sprint, hum or crackle, soar or plummet, purr or sputter, romance or renounce. Why, sometimes the same word can do all of that, depending on how it is used.

Words name persons, preserve history, tag loyalties, pass on faith, welcome guests, direct societies, and contribute to community. That is the positive side of the matter. Words also can depersonalize individuals, scramble corporate memory, foment hatred, raise doubts, demonize enemies, torch covenants, and shred societies. That is the negative.

What would we do without words? Words elaborate ideas, spin tales, raise questions, state convictions, describe beauty, signal fears, deliver information, convey assurance, confess reservations, and establish priorities. Words describe where we live and how to get there, what time it is and what time is for, what we believe and why we believe it. A single word can instruct, discourage, warn, offend, comfort, invite, welcome, exclude, prohibit, or permit.

Words shatter silence and fill space. But, words—at least the most important of them—come from silence. Words emerge from the deep-down silence that nurtures and preserves the recesses of creativity in a person. Words spring from meditation, convictions, study, religion, questions, research, and evaluation. Words take form while listening, working, watching, praying, and playing. Once words emerge from their source in silence and find articulation in the world of sound or print, though, watch out. In the early 1900s, Theobald von Bethmann-Hollweg exclaimed in astonishment, "Just for a word...Great Britain is going to make a war." Words in public reveal attitudes, convey ideas, describe dreams, focus worship, profile doubts, express devotion, pose inquiries, define emotions, and prompt actions both good and bad.

Words delineate identities and differentiate variables of reality. Words position politicians, theologians, and philosophers along an ideological spectrum. Words establish alternative perspectives on current events among journalists, reporters, and commentators. Words spread tales of the ages across pages prepared by distinctly opinionated historians. Words form the testimonies of eyewitnesses who often relay dramatically conflicting accounts of the same event. Words tell the fictional stories of novelists, convey the pleas of beggars, spell out the warnings of prophets, and bear the good tidings of preachers.

Literary geniuses laud the variable nature and awesome vitality of words. Shakespeare wrote of "bitter words" and "unpleasant'st words" declaring his like of "good words" in contrast to an "ill word" with its poisonous influence. Samuel Johnson commented on "uncouth words." Tennyson nodded at "noble words." The author of the biblical Apocalypse commended "true and faithful words" with a force akin to that with which Walter Savage Landin disdained "false words." Oliver Wendell Holmes acknowledged "acrid words" which can "turn the sweet milk of kindness into curds." Conversely, Wordsworth praised "choice words and measured phrases" which rise above the realm of the ordinary. Wentworth Dillon refused to defend "immodest words" perhaps for the same reason that Jesus of Nazareth warned of the judgment evoked by "idle words." All who know words respect their presence and power. In the Hebrew scriptures, one writer characterized good words fitly spoken as "apples of gold in pictures of silver" (Proverbs 25:11, KJV).

In a surgical waiting room, words distinguish the joy-inciting announcement of a benign biopsy from the dreaded confirmation of a malignant mass. In a sales meeting, words celebrate success or bemoan failure. In a relationship, words nurture intimacy or create distance. In contract negotiations, words facilitate a conclusion or break off conversation. In a classroom, words contribute to education or confound ignorance.

When Annie Sullivan accepted the challenge of teaching Helen Keller, who could neither see nor speak, she considered words her greatest allies. To those who inquired as to how she would even begin her work, Annie explained that first, last, and always she would focus on words. This marvelous instructor believed that words would provide Helen Keller eyes to see both inside and outside herself.

Night and day Annie tirelessly spelled words in the palms of her student's hands, carefully using her fingers to sketch the form of each letter. The skilled teacher clung to her strong conviction that a single word could place the world in these same hands. Eventually it happened; a breakthrough occurred. Helen linked the sight of water that poured from a pump with a word spelled in the palm of her hand. At that moment, everything changed. In a very real sense, prompted by recognition of a word, Helen Keller's being emerged.

For Helen Keller, words opened the door to reality and introduced the guest to the hostess. For the rest of us, words do no less.

A STRANGE REQUEST

"Speak but one word to me..."
—WILLIAM MORRIS

*"Words and deeds are quite
indifferent modes of the divine
energy. Words are also actions..."*
—RALPH WALDO EMERSON

"Weigh thy words in a balance."
—ECCLESIASTES 28:25

Convinced of the importance of words, particularly personal words, and impatient about becoming the beneficiary of word gifts from people in all walks of life, how was I to pursue my passion? Taking my cue from that stranger in the story with details I no longer remember, I began asking people if they would give me a word. Like a wide-eyed child eagerly scribbling a wish list for Santa Claus, I made list after list of the names of individuals from whom I wanted to receive a word and then began writing letters to request words from these people. As it turned out, most people did not mind my inquiry. To the contrary, many actually welcomed an opportunity to give away a word and thanked me for asking.

Over the past six years, I have approached many of the most notable people in our society in search of a word. Every one received the same request— "Would you please share with me a word, one of your favorite words, or a brief expression or phrase that you particularly like?" "If you have time," I explained, "I also would appreciate a sentence or two from you explaining why the particular word or phrase you share is important to you."

Responses to these questions fill the pages of this volume. Some individuals offered a single word or phrase, starkly brief but terribly important. Other word-givers provided explanations for the terms or phrases that they chose to share. The result of both is a wonderful collection of word gifts perhaps deserving of Shakespeare's phrase "a rhapsody of words."

In some of the explanations of why a particular word or phrase was especially important to an individual, I personally would have altered the structure of a sentence or chosen a more grammatically preferable format. However, I have recorded the contributors' comments about their words with little or no editing or revision. Faithfully reporting each contributor's word or words prevailed over other concerns.

From the outset of my quest, I anticipated the value of the treasures that I would amass. After all, the offering of a word represents not only a precious gift but a costly form of personal revelation on the part of its giver. Honestly, though, I had no idea of the moving stories, great humor, and profound wisdom that would unfold as contributors explained the importance of the words and phrases that they shared.

WHO SAID WHAT?

"Man's word is God in man."
—ALFRED LORD TENNYSON

*"Words possess primitive mystical incantatory healing powers...
Their articulation represents a complete, lived experience."*
—INGRID BENGIS

Contributors to this collection of words and phrases represent a broad cross-section of the most prominent thinkers, dreamers, entertainers, shakers, shapers, and movers in contemporary society. Most of them, but not all, reside in the United States. Many spend their days in full view of the public's eyes. Several ply their trade through words. Others distinguish themselves by the decisions they make, actions they take, skills they exhibit, or offices they hold rather than by their words.

The gifts on the following pages come from people of a wide range of ages—from Mattie J. T. Stepanek, the young poet, who gave me his word at age eleven, to the now-deceased actor Gregory Peck, who gave me his word late in life; diverse political philosophies—from Republican Mary Matalin, who advises President George W. Bush, to her fiery Democratic consultant husband James Carville; varied religious persuasions—from Mustafa Ceric, the Grand Mufti of Bosnia, to the Dalai Lama of Tibet; competitive social values—from Pat Buchanan to Gloria Steinem; and multiple moral perspectives—from Pat Robertson of the Christian Broadcasting Network to Gene Simmons from the rock group called KISS. Yet, a kindred spirit and mutual sentiments among these people mysteriously weave their patchwork presents into a beautiful linguistic quilt.

I remember vividly the explosion of excitement that I felt when my first word gift from a high-profile person arrived in the mail. The word came from Dick Clark. Here was confirmation for the legitimacy of my question. Now I had no doubts; people really would respond to my request. A collection of word gifts was a viable possibility. A personal dream could become a literary reality.

At no point during this quest for words has my receipt of a new word ever failed to spark enthusiasm. Honestly, though, a few words elicited unique reactions.

One of the most cherished gifts in this volume arrived by mail from the internationally beloved angel of mercy and Nobel Peace Laureate, Mother Teresa of Calcutta. After reading the sensitive offering of this saintly woman, I sat quietly for a long time staring at the paper that held her words, reflecting on her life of compassion as well as her explanation of the significance of her prayerful terms. A profound sense of reverence and an overwhelming rush of gratitude swept over me during those moments, penetrating to the core of my being.

Another word gift of special import came as a result of a personal visit with its benefactor. One sweltering summer day in the little fishing village of Cojimar, Cuba, I sat in a small un-air-conditioned room listening intently to Ernest Hemingway's best friend reminisce about the great author and their exploits together. Gregorio Fuentes served as captain of Hemingway's prized boat *Pilar*. When I asked the ninety-nine years of age man if he could guess what Hemingway's favorite word might have been, he answered quickly and confidently, "Peace." Then the old man of the sea shared with me another word—his own favorite word.

Some recipients of my request for a word responded immediately. Larry King read my request for a word while sitting behind his desk in Los Angeles only minutes before going on the air to do another installment of *Larry King Live*. No sooner did he finish reading my letter than the internationally acclaimed television personality promptly wrote down his response and handed it to me. Former senator Bob Kerrey and I met in the cramped commuter terminal of an international airport, each of us on our way to a meeting at which both of us were to speak. Squatting against a wall, the Senator read my letter and quickly scribbled his response—a word gift that reflected an internal struggle of his that had, in recent days, become a part of the front-page script of newspapers across the land. When former president Gerald Ford and I talked about my search for word gifts in his home in Colorado, he told me what he thought he wanted to share with me as his word offering, though he requested time to ponder his response. In the end, President Ford gave me exactly the same words that comprised his initial thoughts in response to my request.

Other recipients of my request for a word wanted time for reflection—such a length of time, in some instances, that I thought I never was going to receive their words. Dixie Carter reflected on her response for weeks. One evening after Ms. Carter had played the starring role in *Master Class* on Broadway, my wife and I visited her backstage. Right away, she explained that she had been thinking about "her word" for weeks and that she had made a decision. Then, with a teasing smile on her face, Ms. Carter told me that she wanted me to read her gift rather than hear it from her that evening. Later that same week, during an appearance on *Late Night with David Letterman*, Ms. Carter talked with Mr. Letterman about the challenge of deciding on her word gift. Similarly, Judith Light took months to respond to my request, not because she did not want to give me a word, but because, true to her characteristic compassion and integrity, Ms. Light wanted to share a word that really mattered to her.

Readers of this volume will discover gifts from actors who have been recognized with a Tony, an Oscar, or an Emmy; Pulitzer Prize-winning writers including syndicated columnists and best-selling authors; musicians honored by multiple awards—like a Grammy—and blessed by loyal fans; members of sports halls of fame and active athletes who set the standards for their competitors; artists whose works adorn galleries around the world; politicians who have served or serve at the highest levels of government; educators whose contributions to the worlds of research and learning defy description; business executives who guide the largest, most effective corporations around the globe; physicians who chart new paths in the diagnosis and treatment of diseases; social activists who have altered the face of a community or changed the course of a nation; religious leaders whose priestly and prophetic words and deeds help shape the spirituality of scores of people; and Nobel Laureates in a variety of fields.

Not everyone from whom I requested a word responded positively or even responded. A lack of interest, a shortage of time, or contractual restrictions prohibited several persons from participating in this project. For others, sharing a word simply was not their "thing." Obviously, though, many people generously offered a word or phrase of personal meaning and thereby graced me, and now us, with no small gifts.

I GIVE YOU MY WORD

Deep into my search for words from a variety of people, mail time each day took on the character of the appointed hour for a long-anticipated birthday party. Like a fidgety-with-excitement child eager to open wished-for gifts, I looked forward to sorting through a stack of envelopes to see if any one of them contained a word forwarded to me. Every time a word gift arrived, I felt a strange sense of honor and a surge of the emotion that feeds a celebration.

I treasure every word gift that I have received over the past several years and live with gratitude for the generous donors. Often, when I read of the death of someone to whom I had directed a request for a word gift but from whom I had not received a response, I find myself grieving that I missed knowing something important about that individual. Conversely, when I read the obituary of a person who shared a word with me, I breathe a prayer of thankfulness, feeling that I am the beneficiary of a gift from that person that will live on despite the individual's death. Indeed, the people who have sent words to me have engaged in a kind of self-revelation that established a strange bond between us, a bond that transcends a physical meeting between us.

My friend Rev. Dr. Fred B. Craddock is a Christian minister widely renowned for his rhetorical agility and his unique ability to teach others how to speak. Frequently politicians and other professionals who rely heavily on the power of words seek out Fred's counsel, knowing full well that the manner in which they pronounce a word or turn a phrase may spell the difference between winning or losing an election, closing a business deal or seeing its rewards claimed by someone else. One morning at the Chautauqua Institution in Chautauqua, New York, I listened with surprise and delight as, in a sermonic address, Fred reflected on his respect for the power of words and his interest in the use of words—verbs "busy doing their thing without calling attention to themselves;" nouns that "stand straight up and come marching" out of one's mouth; participles "meandering through a sentence, flavoring it." The closing sentences of Fred's superb address intersected my long search for a title under which to publish this collection of word gifts. Lights flashed in my mind and adrenalin rushed through my body as, unexpectedly, this good friend handed to me that for which I had been searching. Bringing to a close his remarks addressed to an audience of influential leaders in varied segments of society, Fred pleaded with his listeners to give to their families, to their children, to their communities, to their religious institutions, and to their nation the only real gift that, in his opinion, they had to offer—the gift of their word. At that moment the conclusion to my friend's sermon served as the inspiration for the title given to this collection. Citing the phrase "I give you my word," Dr. Fred B. Craddock observed, "'I give you my word' is the raw material for the revival and reformation of our country."

With such high hopes and exalted expectations for words, I am pleased to share with you the words that have been given to me, words that have become a part of my life and thought. I offer these words now as gifts to you!

WORD GIFTS

ACCOUNTABILITY

It is the essence of representative government, and it also describes the sense of personal responsibility for the actions and behavior that are the heart of our personal lives.

DAVID S. BRODER
National Political Correspondent and Syndicated Columnist
The Washington Post

ADVERSITY

THE SWEET USES OF ADVERSITY

When a door closes, it often allows other doors to open—if only we look for them. I experienced this and it enriched my life.

I believe the phrase is from a Shakespeare play, but I can't tell you which one. Another simpler way to put this is Johnny Mercer's "Accentuate the Positive!"

MARSHA HUNT
Actor

AFRAID

AT THIS MOMENT, GENTLEMEN, I THINK THAT
YOU ARE MORE AFRAID OF ME THAN I OF YOU.

Response of Giordano Bruno to the sentence of death by fire
delivered to him on 9th February 1600; report by the German,
Kasper Schoppe (who was present on the occasion).

MORRIS L. WEST
Author

AL-HAQQ

The Arabic word "al-Haqq" means "Truth." It also means "Right," as in human rights. It is the foundation of Justice, and hence a law school in the Arab World is usually called "Masrassat al-Huquq" (School of Rights).

Yet, al-Haqq is not a legal tool I wield against others. It is a worldview that commits me to protect you, and others I may have never met or seen, even from my own prejudices, greed, and lust for power.

"Al-Haqq" is one of God's beautiful names. For in God there is not distinction between Justice, Truth, and Beauty.

DR. AZIZAH Y. AL-HIBRI
Professor of Law, Specialist in Islamic Law (Sharia)
T. C. Williams School of Law, The University of Richmond
Founder of KARAMAH

AMAZE

DON'T FULFILL MY EXPECTATIONS—AMAZE ME!

This is what I want from people who call for my attention and, as an editorial cartoonist, this is what I hope the readers ask me.

RIBER HANSSON
Editorial Cartoonist
Sweden

AMAZING

Some love to demoralize,
I respond and am energized by the wonder of my life.
Amazing grace and love are mine.

JESSIE COLTER
Country Music Singer

5

AND YET

Often we love now, and yet we must reinvent it.

ELIE WIESEL
Andrew W. Mellon Professor in the Humanities
University Professor, Boston University
Author
Nobel Peace Laureate, 1986

ANTHROPOCENE

THE ANTHROPOCENE: HUMAN-CAUSED GEOLOGY

It underlines the major impact many major human activities have
on the earth's environment and biogeochemical cycles.

PROFESSOR DR. PAUL J. CRUTZEN
Emeritus Professor, Utrecht University Institute for Marine and
Atmospheric Sciences
The Netherlands
Nobel Laureate in Chemistry, 1995

APPRECIATION

APPRECIATION AND RESPONSIBILITY, THE AIM AND MEASURE OF EDUCATION

To fail or be deprived in the development of either is to be limited, crippled, or dysfunctional in life.

Appreciation is to gain. The ability to respond is to live, as contrasted with limited existence.

Responsibility is not to be limited to or confused with "obligation."

THE RIGHT REVEREND JOHN W. ALLIN
Former Presiding Bishop
The Episcopal Church, USA

APPROPRIATE

It's so helpful in so many situations and mature.

ANGIE DICKINSON
Actor

ARMY

AN ARMY OF LIONS LED BY A DEER
WILL ALWAYS BE DEFEATED BY
AN ARMY OF DEER LED BY A LION.

The above phrase is an Arabic saying about the power and
importance of leadership.

STONE PHILLIPS
Television Journalist, NBC-TV
Dateline NBC

ART

Art adds immeasurably to the lives of individuals.
Art is important to society because it is such a civilizing force.
Art is such an important part of education.
                    And
Art should be important to us because it really is our most
lasting legacy.

John H. Bryan
Chief Executive Officer
Sara Lee Corporation

ASK

IF YOU HAVE TO ASK, YOU'LL NEVER MAKE IT.

The above was the normal response of George Burns and I totally
agree. It has to come from within and the want to's have to be
there real bad.

Mel Tillis
Country Music Singer

ATTITUDE

With the proper attitude, it allows one to experience the failures of life and move on. It also lets one experience success, promotions, and awards with the appropriate positive.

WILLIAM J. KNIGHT
Astronaut, X-15 Pilot
Set record for altitude

ATTITUDE

It is within my personal control and it directly impacts every relationship/personal contact I maintain. An appropriate attitude, negative or positive, will always enable clarity of self-perception and communication.

HENRY B. SMITH
President and Chief Executive Officer
Bank of Bermuda Limited
Bermuda

ATTITUDE

ATTITUDE AND PERSEVERANCE

Attitude and perseverance are interchangeable when determining how a person looks at life. As we approach a new millennium, the circumstances we all encounter are getting harder to face. Once a person develops the proper attitude to take on any and all challenges, it then takes perseverance to make it through any difficult time. Combining these words all add up to one thing: making a difference in society. As a leader of a large urban police department such as ours, this overall philosophy is something which keeps me focused as I carry out my daily functions to the best of my **ability**.

I am looked upon each day to lead this organization in a forward and progressive direction. As I continue to spread the message of "**attitude and perseverance**" to all members of this department, I expect those under my leadership to understand this philosophy and apply it. Over time this feeling spreads, to the point where we are all trying to make a difference to the public we serve.

RICHARD J. PENNINGTON
Chief of Police
Atlanta, Georgia

AUDACITY

Any famous coaches, generals, officers, etc. stood above the others because of their audaciousness. They "dared" to do it when others said, "You wouldn't dare try it!"

BOBBY BOWDEN
Head Football Coach
Florida State University

AUTHENTICITY

I believe, for me, that authenticity is a powerful word.
It encompasses many feelings and other words such as integrity, honesty, being real in everything you do in this life and being, most importantly, an authentic person with or to yourself.
Reliable, trustworthy—not false or copied but genuine.

MARGE RIVINGSTON
Musician, Voice Coach for the stars

BALANCE

Many of us struggle much of the time to find the appropriate balance between working but conflicting objectives. God and the world, prayer and action, work and family, solitude and involvement, pleasure and need, saving versus charity, leisure and ambition, etc., etc.

Like the "Fiddler on the Roof," keeping our balance is usually difficult, but always essential. Practice helps, and sometimes, even as we teeter, we can also create beauty and joy.

ROBERT C. ABERNETHY
Executive Editor and Host
Religion and Ethics Newsweekly, Public Broadcasting System

BE

BE YOURSELF.

"Inch by inch, life's a cinch
Yard by yard, it's really hard."
This is the way life really is. I have found it to be a great
guide for mine.

MORGAN WOOTEN
Former Boys' Basketball Coach at Damatha High School
Baltimore, Maryland

BEAUTY

One of my favorite quotes is "Let the beauty we love be what we
do." (Rumi) I find this very true with me—for dance!

HOLLY CRUIKSHANK
Dancer on Broadway

BELIEVE

ALICE WALKER
Author

BEST

SIMPLY DO **YOUR** VERY BEST.

This is what I expect of others—and this is what I strive to do myself.

TOM JOHNSON
Retired Chairman and Chief Executive Officer
CNN News Group

BETTER

EACH OF US PASSES THROUGH THIS LIFE ONLY ONCE.
IT IS MY HOPE THAT WHEN I LEAVE, THIS WORLD
WILL BE A BETTER PLACE BECAUSE I WAS THERE.

I am taking the liberty of sending you the enclosed statement
which I have repeated many times, particularly during my "senior
years." I recognize that it is more lengthy than a "word" or
"phrase." As you probably are aware, this statement is a direct
quote from the famous Quaker, William Penn.

ROBERT J. LIPSHUTZ
Lipshutz, Greenblatt & King
White House Lawyer for President Jimmy Carter

BIRD

A WET BIRD NEVER FLIES AT NIGHT.

It can be used whenever you feel you are in danger of saying anything important, whenever anyone asks for a dance, when you need a moment to collect your thoughts.

LESLIE NIELSEN
Actor

BLESSINGS

I sign autographs with this sentiment because I hope to be a blessing to other people's lives. My life has certainly been blessed and, as you might guess, has much to do with my spiritual side. It makes me hope that others have faith in something higher.

LOU DIAMOND PHILLIPS
Actor

BOMBASTIC

RAPID FIRE, EFFERVESCENT, BREEZY,
MACHINE GUN, STACCATO, FAST, FIERY, FURIOUS

I've always hated those references when describing my performances.
They always left out witty, sharp, incisive, intelligent, creative,
perceptive, and awesome! They would always discuss my speed of
performance as energy and nothing more. It's the old joke or saying:
But the audience loved him. Had to beg off!

JACK CARTER
Comedian

BRAINS

HE WHO HAS THE BRAINS TO CRITICIZE SHOULD
HAVE THE HEART TO HELP.

I offer this phrase to you because it captures the truth that the
ultimate responsibility is to care for others with all the gifts and
talents (brains) one has received.

AART J. DE GEUS
Chairman and Chief Executive Officer, Synopsys Inc.

BREATHE

It is useful when things are going well or badly.

JAMIE LEE CURTIS
Actor

BRIDGE

The concept of bridging differences in the search for common ground has been at the center of my entire creative life. Starting in college as a student body officer at U.C. Berkeley, a campus divided between the "Greeks" and the "Independents," on to Korea as a military government officer north of the 38th Parallel, sharing government responsibility with my Korean counterpart, and then the Peace Corps for seven years that included being on the United States United Nations delegation to ECOSOC, my challenge was always bridging cultures or languages, ideology or geography, to find ways to work toward shared goals. When I then went to build an international think tank in academia (The Adlai Stevenson Institute at the University of Chicago), followed by directing international activities for Xerox Corporation, and later running a public policy forum (The American Assembly based at Columbia University), that sought consensus among national and world leaders, the constantly helpful image for me was always a bridge: how to bridge the differences to move forward. Now I am applying this concept in the creation of two new international structures, The Club of Madrid that is reaching for agreement on strengthening democracy among country presidents, and the Royal Institution World Science Assembly (RiSci) that is seeking global consensus at the highest levels on today's most critical issues driven by science and technology.

DANIEL A. SHARP
President & Chief Executive Officer
Royal Institution World Science Assembly

BROTHERHOOD

Brotherhood is the bond we enter into when we become firefighters. Never has it been more profoundly honored than in the aftermath of 9/11.

WILLIAM KING
Firefighter, Engine Company 6
New York Fire Department
First Company to the World Trade Towers on 9/11/01

BUSINESS

Some people would say our business is selling soft drinks. I would say our business is building relationships.

After more than 30 years working for this Company, it is clear to me that these relationships must be based on mutual benefit, trust, and shared values.

Our business succeeds or fails based on our ability to build and nourish billions of relationships every day, making a tangible contribution to the lives of everyone our business touches.

DOUG DAFT
Chairman and Chief Executive Officer
The Coca-Cola Company

CAN

YOU CAN.

I firmly believe that whatever you can dream can be accomplished if you plan thoroughly enough, work hard enough. You can do it. You can.

JENNIFER BLAKE
Author

CANDLE

TO EXTINGUISH ANOTHER'S CANDLE WILL NOT MAKE YOURS SHINE ANY BRIGHTER.

Years ago I was picking up my car, which had been left at my local mechanic's garage for repair. While waiting to pick it up, I noticed an inexpensive calendar hanging on the wall, given to the garage by one of their suppliers. It had a "phrase of the month" on each page and as I glanced at that month's phrase, I doubted I would find it particularly noteworthy. But, I was wrong. It said, "To extinguish another's candle will not make yours shine any brighter."

In all facets of my life, as a business leader, husband, father, friend, following this phrase's instruction has stopped me from being petty and churlish. And I have been struck by how many other people could benefit from following its simple prescription for life. Perhaps it will be meaningful to your readers.

BRUCE L. CLAFLIN
President and Chief Executive Officer
3Com Corporation

CAN'T

THE MAN WHO SAYS IT CAN'T BE DONE IS ALWAYS
INTERRUPTED BY THE MAN WHO JUST DID IT.

I didn't originate this—but I try to live by it!

MICKEY SPILLANE
Author, Producer

CARING

If we begin with caring for others it could avoid many of
our problems.

CHARLES GRODIN
Actor, Television Personality

CARING

CARING AND DOING.

Not enough people care about problems they are aware of, whether the problems be moral values or political situations, and whether they be in the community, the country, or the world... and most of those who are aware and care, think about it, feel it, and discuss it "around the dinner table," but don't get in there and do something about it.

ARTHUR HILLER
Movie Director

CHARACTER

YOU CAN MEASURE THE CHARACTER OF AN
INDIVIDUAL OR AN INSTITUTION BY THE
WAY THEY TREAT DEFENSELESS PERSONS.

This is a sentence which has shaped my life. I have always been sensitive to the vulnerable and unprotected. At the age of 10 I saw a teenager shoot a black man walking down Main Street of our small town with a sling shot loaded with a "cork" (a piece of metal cut from a horseshoe). The man expressed extreme pain but didn't dare retaliate or even protest. To do so may have cost him his life. For in 1921 blacks in my hometown were segregated and not permitted in town after dark.

As a child of 13, I worked in cotton mills in the South 10 hours per day 5 1/2 days per week for 18 cents per hour. Retirement benefits, adequate medical care, and job security were unknown. People could be dismissed from their jobs for no reason at all.

I know a widow who worked 60 years in the cotton mill until she could no longer do the hard work. Her retirement fund was inadequate to meet her basic needs. Her son paid the rent until she died.

Today popular people in sports and business are getting rich off the hard labor of children. Exposés by the media reveal that this practice flourishes not only in foreign countries but occurs in the United States.

Some religious institutions take advantage of employees. A charge of heresy is used as a political tool to displace persons who, on grounds of conscience, refuse to conform to authoritarian ecclesiocrats and their erroneous edicts.

God, if we believe the Bible, is on the side of the defenseless, especially that of the poor, the widows, the orphans, the children. These are those who cannot fight back and defend themselves. So, God, through His stout-hearted and strong ones, stands up for the weak (James 1:27).

DR. HENLEE H. BARNETTE
Christian Ethicist, Expert in Medical Ethics, Author

CHARACTER

Character is knowing what is RIGHT and then doing what is RIGHT, not about popularity - politically correct or finding favor. It's about right and wrong in the eyes of God.

MIKE DITKA
Television Commentator
Former National Football League Head Coach
Chicago Bears, New Orleans Saints

CHERISH

The best artistic credo I ever saw was the late composer Lou Harrison's four-word motto, "Cherish, conserve, consider, create." He understood that all worthwhile creation begins in deep and abiding affection for the medium in which one works. It has long been evident to me that much of life works in this same way. Our best accomplishments begin in the impulse of love and the need to protect, foster, and preserve what we behold closest to our hearts.

DANA GIOIA
Chairman of the National Endowment for the Arts

CHERISH

Love is nice, but to be cherished is even better.

EDWARD ASNER
Actor

CHILDHOOD

I HAD A HAPPY CHILDHOOD.

It is true, and made my life wonderful, carefree and confident, for as long as I remember.

MAEVE BINCHY
Irish Author

CHILDREN

TO THE CHILDREN OF THE SEVENTH GENERATION!

As leaders of our Handemosaunee Nations, we are required by the great law of Peace to keep the children of the Seventh Generation in mind when making decisions in council.

CHIEF JAKE SWAMP
Founder of The Tree of Peace Society
Author of children's books

CHOICE

Choice implies self-authority and the power to exercise it, whether in the choice to have children or not, and marry or not, or the choice of leaders to vote for in a democracy. It is not just individual, but also the right to form communities with collective choice. Thus, choice can be both a declaration of independence and a declaration of interdependence.

GLORIA STEINEM
Feminist Leader
Editor of *Ms. Magazine*

CHOICE

I work with the Republican Pro-Choice Coalition and I passionately believe in a woman's right to "choose" when and if she wants to give birth. Children who are not wanted should not be forced into our world. Every child deserves and needs love. So, I'm for "choice"!

DINA MERRILL
Actor

CHOICES

LIFE IS FULL OF CHOICES. MAKE THEM.

So many people dodge responsibility and whine.
Face up and decide.

KAREN ELLIOTT HOUSE
President
Dow Jones & Company International

CHRIST

CHRIST LIVES

The fact that Christ died for my sake, was buried, and rose to live has become the center of my life since the day when he touched my heart. It makes me see everything in my life as a gift from him, worthy of respect and love, and it gives sense to my life, because I know that I will live with him. It is also an important inspiration for an economist, because it encourages us to use the resources Christ has entrusted to us wisely and efficiently.

DR. JUERGEN VON HAGEN
Professor of Economics, Center for European Integration Studies
University of Bonn

CLASS

I have always tried to behave with class.

DICK VAN PATTEN
Actor

CLICHÉS

TO ME THERE ARE TWO OLD CLICHÉS THAT
SAY IT ALL:

1. TO THINE OWNSELF BE TRUE.
2. THE ONLY WAY TO FAIL IS TO QUIT.

A. SCOTT CROSSFIELD
Pilot of the first X-15 flight, June 8, 1959

COCA-COLA

With warmest personal regards.

ROBERTO C. GOIZUETA
Former Chairman of the Board and Chief Executive Officer
The Coca-Cola Company

COMMANDMENT

ONE COMMANDMENT FITS ALL
THOU SHALT NOT HURT—ANYBODY!

CARL REINER
Emmy Award-Winning Comedian, Actor,
Novelist, and Film Director
Creator, Writer, and Producer of *The Dick Van Dyke Show*

COMMIT

IN ANY LIFE ENDEAVOR, ONE MUST
COMMIT THE PIG.

When thinking about bacon and eggs,
The chicken is involved,
The pig is committed.

GIGI FERNANDEZ
Professional Tennis Player

COMMITMENT

Without it dreams become meaningless.

CAPTAIN EUGENE A. CERNAN
Astronaut, *Gemini IX, Gemini X, Apollo 10, Apollo 17*

COMMITMENT

Winners make commitments.
Losers make excuses.

JOHN SCHUERHOLZ
General Manager
Atlanta Braves Major League Baseball Team

COMMITMENT

To be a good coach...player...employee...parent...child...you must be committed. You must promise...pledge...obligate yourself... to be the best you can be.

PAT HEAD SUMMIT
Head Coach, Women's Basketball
University of Tennessee
Member of the Naismith Basketball Hall of Fame (since 2000)

COMMON SENSE

Common sense will result in the understanding of differing points of view and in the retention of dignity.

DR. WENDELIN WIEDEKING
President and Chief Executive Officer
Porsche AG
Germany

COMMUNITY

It suggests togetherness and unity. With that theme the building of spirits, relationships, and wholeness can happen and then justice will prevail.

SANFORD CLOUD
President and Chief Executive Officer
The National Conference for Community and Justice

COMPASSION

Compassion is the basis of all good deeds.

HIS HOLINESS THE DALAI LAMA

COMPASSION

Understanding and caring about the plight of others—giving of
yourself to help those in difficulties—emotional or physical.
The rewards are great—in showing that you care.

ELI WALLACH
Actor

COMPASSION

Compassion—sums up—in one word—through faith—life—and
cultures—all that is good and right.

BILL MITCHELL
Clothier

COMPASSION

If we all had it for each other we would begin to heal the hurts of
the planet, one heart at a time.

LUCIE ARNAZ
Actor

COMPASSION

I feel we are at the most dangerous time in human history. Money and power over time became our value system and in the U.S. created a fascist government that is a puppet to money and power. It has led to a schoolteacher (second in importance only to mother in human life) being barely able to support their family and a ball player being a multi-millionaire. The 35,000 children that die of starvation a day and the billion people with no access to water are also consequences. Compassion for all is the answer.

PATCH ADAMS, M.D.
Medical Doctor, Clown, Social Activist
Founder and Director of the Gesundheit Institute
Subject of the hit movie *Patch Adams* starring Robin Williams

COMPETITIVE
(COMPETITOR)

I offer this word to you because of the desire to be the best.

ROBERT HUGHES
Head Coach, Boys' Basketball
Dunbar High School, Fort Worth, Texas
Winningest coach in the history of United States boys' basketball

CONDUIT

It has been my privilege and distinct pleasure to be a conduit for people of a great variety of different religions, cultures, and nations to come together. In doing so, these people have gotten to know one another, to appreciate one another's values and differences. So they have grown in understanding, ignorance of what is different has been dispelled, as has the fear which ignorance can create. The world is better served when such things happen and I am indeed honored to have been one of the conduits for such work. The one Creator of us all is also better served. I am grateful.

ELIZABETH ESPERSEN
Former Executive Vice President and Executive Director
Center for World Thanksgiving

CONFIDENCE

CONFIDENCE IN THE UNLIMITED RESOURCES
OF LIFE

I believe spiritual growth is a continual challenge in daily life that requires exercising faith and courage as a force of progress, and never tolerates conforming or defeat.

MARTHA I. RUIZ CORZO
Director, Sierra Gorda Biosphere Reserve
Planted one million trees last year
Mexico

CONNECTIONS

About half of the people in the world have never even used a telephone. Think about that. Half of the world cut off from a device that's so much a part of our daily lives. And cut off, as a result, from a lot of other things we also take for granted...like education and health care.

And so, from our perspective, the challenge is not just to build networks. It's to build connections with those communities who have been isolated from technology, and thus cut off from economic opportunity.

Building those connections is what SBC is all about in places like South Africa, where we'll be helping to meet an almost overwhelming demand for telephone service in a new partnership with South Africa's national telephone company, Telkom. It's what we're about in Mexico, where we've helped our partner Telmex bring telephone service—for the first time—to thousands of rural towns. Just as important, though, we are committed to keep building connections right here at home...whether it's through new products and services for our customers...good jobs to support our local economies...or millions of hours given by company volunteers to support the special needs of our communities.

When I think of the work yet to be done to connect millions more people to new opportunities—I know the journey has just begun.

ED WHITACRE
Chairman and Chief Executive Officer
SBC Communications, Inc.

CONSCIENCE

CONSCIENCE GIVES PEOPLE AN INNATE SENSE OF
RIGHT FROM WRONG.

Compassion identifies a person with sympathy for fellow human
beings—humanity.

These words—conscience, compassion, humanity—lay the
foundation for the phrase:

"No man is an island," or "we are our brother's keeper."

HELEN THOMAS
Senior White House Correspondent
Syndicated Columnist, Hearst Newspapers
"Dean of the Washington Press Corps"
Traditionally asks the first question at a presidential press conference
Author

CONSISTENT

It's my conviction that "consistent" is a very important word because the only way we build long-term relationships and long-term successes is with consistency. We should be in private what we appear to be in public. I've had two highly visible public figures who really disappointed me early in my career. They were one thing publicly and another privately.

At that point I decided that if I ever achieved any success in my life, I would work overtime to be consistent in what I appear to be and in what I am.

ZIG ZIGLAR
Author, Motivational Speaker
Ziglar Training Systems
Expert on Success

CONSTANT

SEAN CONNERY
Actor, 1997 Academy Award for his performance in *The Untouchables*
1998 British Academy of Film and Television Arts, Lifetime
Achievement Award

CONSTRUCTIVELY DISSATISFIED

Our competitive world calls for continual improvement.
Those companies who don't improve service and/or products
will disappear. "Constructive dissatisfaction" recognized a need to
continually look for a better way, but keeping in mind that change
and any criticism of old ways should be done in a positive way.
It expresses an attitude of building on old strengths rather than
tearing down old outdated ideas.

KENT C. NELSON
Retired President and Chief Executive Officer
United Parcel Service

CONTEXT

WENDELL BERRY
Author, Poet, Environmentalist, Social Activist

COOKING

COOKING IS AN ACT OF KINDNESS, WHEN CARING IS WRAPPED IN PLEASURE.

It underlines my mission in this frantic world where we are beginning to believe those who wish us to consume more—that we have less time.

Eventually we begin to run out of time to be kind...what a tragic end to our culture when we too are consumed...by **it**!

GRAHAM KERR
Chef
Television Personality
"The Galloping Gourmet"

COOL

A COOL HEAD AND A WARM HEART

I have found this phrase apt in describing the qualities a judge or others in authority should have.

JUSTICE SANDRA DAY O'CONNOR
United States Supreme Court Justice
First Woman Appointed to the United States Supreme Court

COOL

BE COOL.

My interpretation of being cool is to be yourself, not get into playing roles or trying to be cool.

ELMORE LEONARD
Author

COURAGE

I believe it to be one of the most important virtues. Without courage no one can practice the other virtues consistently. One cannot be consistently kind, courteous, generous, fair, merciful, or loving without courage.

MAYA ANGELOU
Author, Poet
1993 Inaugural Poet

COURAGE

I believe that courage is the quality that allows us to overcome obstacles, pressures, failures and even success to:
> Do the **right** thing
> **Earn** what we get
> Take responsibility for all our actions

LANCE BROWN
Former Head Coach, Men's Baseball Team
Texas Christian University

COURAGE

It seems to me to be in dreadfully short supply in our world, and in the Church. As to a word of explanation, it is II Timothy 1:7 "...for God did not give us a spirit of timidity but a spirit of power and love and self-control."

RICHARD JOHN NEUHAUS
Author
President of Religion and Public Life

COURAGE

It's said to be the virtue that makes all other virtues possible.

DAVID MCCULLOUGH
Author, 1993 Pulitzer for *Truman*
Expert on Leadership

COVENANT

No covenant is as important to the future of humankind
as to translate will and resources into action against poverty
and social injustice.

JAMES D. WOLFENSOHN
President of The World Bank

CRADLE

It is both a noun and a verb.
It implies a motion of the body and the act of nurturing.
It is both abstract and concrete.

PATTIANN ROGERS
Author

CREATE

It applies to everything in life and the concept of it keeps me alive as an artist and as a human being.

JENNA ELFMAN
Actor, Dharma in ABC-TV's *Dharma & Greg*

CREATION

Eating, dining, food, survival, history, art, passion, future vision, life. All make up part of what I do every day. The "creation" of food— direct from the farmer who grew it from the seed—the farmer who helps nurse and care for the cattle or the worker who hand-harvests cocoa beans from their branch all play a part in today's Food Arts. One of the most complex, time-consuming, visually satisfying, and energizing forms of art there is. Truly the most diverse medium, cooking, is my life's work, and I'm just getting started.

TORY L. MCPHAIL
Chef, Commander's Palace
New Orleans, Louisiana

CREATIVE

If you're creative you can turn sad into happy,
a cloudy day to a sunny day,
hate into love, suspicion into trust.
It may take a bit of practice, but you can do it.

BUCK OWENS
Country Music Singer
Television Entertainer

CREATIVITY

My whole life has been devoted to the development of what I have
discovered through the study of Scientology which addresses the
very core of life—and that is every person's native creative ability.

CHICK COREA
Pianist, Jazz Musician, Composer

CURIOSITY

Because I'm nothing if not curious, and have been all my life. It's still what drives me to do the research I do to write the kind of books that I do.

JEAN AUEL
Author, *Earth's Children Series* (5 volumes)

DADDY

The word "Daddy," as said by a small girl, is the sweetest and most pleasant sound in the world to me.
(Being a father and a grandfather, I've heard it a lot, and it still melts me!)

GREGORY WALCOTT
Actor, Author

DECENCY

I know many people who are very smart and many people who are very talented, but I know all too few people to whom being decent to other people is their central moral commitment. Social life is possible only if we encounter one another with a commitment to make life possible for the other.

RABBI ARTHUR HERTZBERG
Author, Rabbi Emeritus of Temple Emanu-El
Englewood, New Jersey
Bronfman Visiting Professor of the Humanities,
New York University

DEMOCRACY

"MAN'S CAPACITY FOR JUSTICE MAKES DEMOCRACY
POSSIBLE, BUT MAN'S INCLINATION TO INJUSTICE
MAKES DEMOCRACY NECESSARY."
—Reinhold Niebuhr
The Children of Light and the Children of Darkness

Alas, I am unable to think of a single word that illuminates my
life. If you are in the market for sentences, I would offer Reinhold
Niebuhr's powerful declaration.

ARTHUR SCHLESINGER JR.
Author

DESOLATION

MAGNIFICENT DESOLATION

As I first stepped onto the moon, I looked at its surface and
remarked, "Beautiful. Beautiful. Magnificent desolation."

BUZZ ALDRIN
Astronaut, *Apollo 11*

DETERMINATION

Bulldog determination is the key to helping make your dreams come true.

DICK CLARK
Television Personality, Producer

DETERMINATION

Determination is the key to success. Why? Because nothing can be achieved without the determination to see a task through to its end, and the determination to devote your full ability to any challenge.

LUCIO A. NOTO
Former Chairman and Chief Executive Officer
Mobil Corporation

DEVOTION

Devotion to principle, to an ideal, to our work, and most especially to one's **few** who mean the **most**—one's mate, one's children, parents, family, and friends, if we be lucky enough to have **real** friends. We cannot be truly devoted to very many people or endeavors. True devotion is the goal of my life. I have received and I hope to return it.

DIXIE CARTER
Actor

DIALOGUE

NEVER BEFORE HAS THE WORLD BEEN SO
IN NEED FOR DIALOGUE AND COOPERATION.

JOSE MARIA FIGUERES
Senior Managing Director, The World Economic Forum
Former President of Costa Rica

DIFFERENCE

MAKE A DIFFERENCE.

Every human being must strike to change things for the better for fellow human beings. With example and credibility of purpose, he should "make a difference" in the lives of others.

IKRAM UL-MAJEED SEHGAL
Managing Director, Pathfinder Group
Pakistan

DIGNITY

DIGNITY AND TENACITY OR PERSEVERANCE

I think what keeps us going in adverse times is keeping our dignity and persevering in our goals.

NORA LUSTIG
Rector/President, Universidad de las Américas
Puebla, Mexico

DISCOMBOBULATE

I was about 14 years old in high school when I first heard this word and immediately knew it was meant to signify confusion, five bouncy syllables shaking one's beliefs around. I thought then it was the kind of slang that wouldn't find its way into a dictionary but I'm pleased to note it has *(Concise Oxford)*. As a cartoonist, I often push scenarios to extremes to make a point about current reality, but often the world is so crazy that reality overtakes the cartoons and becomes more bizarre than anything I can think of. *That's* when I feel discombobulated.

JONATHAN ZAPIRO
Editorial Cartoonist, Zaprock Productions
South Africa

DO

DO UNTO OTHERS AS YOU WOULD HAVE THEM
DO UNTO YOU.

GENERAL WILLIAM C. WESTMORELAND
United States Army

DO

WHAT I'VE DREAMED, I'VE WILLED.
WHAT I'VE WILLED, I'LL DO.

It defines succinctly the "conscious act" Thoreau made reference to
as necessary to elevating our mortal prolusion.

TODD CHRISTENSEN
Former Player in the National Football League
Oakland Raiders
Sports Commentator, NBC-TV

DO

WHAT YOU DO SPEAKS SO LOUD
NO NEED TO HEAR WHAT YOU SAY.

Be an example by how you carry yourself!

DAN REEVES
Head Coach in the National Football League
Formerly of the Denver Broncos and New York Giants
Presently of the Atlanta Falcons

DO

WHATEVER YOU DO IN LIFE,
DO IT FOR THE LOVE OF DOING IT.

It has served me well in life.

WAYNE M. ROGERS
Actor, Writer, Director of M*A*S*H

DOGMA

It shows how far Western Christianity has diverged from other faiths in its rationalistic approach. For the Greek Orthodox, **dogma** is everything about religion which cannot be explained, defined, or understood rationally, but which can only be grasped intuitively, spiritually, and apophetically. In the West, it means quite the opposite.

KAREN ARMSTRONG
Author, A History of God
United Kingdom

DOUBT

It's the watchword of my favor, which is that nothing should be taken on favor, but should be analyzed, dissected, questioned, toppled, and sometimes even affirmed.

DANIEL LAZARE
Author

DOUBT

Doubt—organized skepticism—is the defining characteristic of modern science. Insofar as a person takes anything on faith, that person is not being a scientist in that respect. Since I believe science is one of man's highest callings, I offer the word which stands for it.

PHILIP W. ANDERSON
Nobel Laureate in Physics, 1977

DREAM

I believe to live your potential to its fullest, you must see beyond what's right in front of you. You must challenge yourself to **dream** with your imagination so you can create a more fulfilling reality.

SHARON LAWRENCE
Actor, *NYPD Blue, Ladies Man*

DREAM

This word, used so powerfully by Dr. Martin Luther King Jr., is one I often use when speaking to gay and lesbian audiences, daring them to dream of, then create, a world in which we are free.
"If you dream of a world in which you can put your partner's picture on your desk, then put his picture on your desk...and you will live in such a world.

"And if you dream of a world in which you can walk down the street holding your partner's hand, then hold her hand...and you will live in such a world.

"If you dream of a world in which there are more openly gay elected officials, then run for office...and you will live in such a world. And if you dream of a world in which you can take your partner to the office party, even if your office is the U.S. House of Representatives, then take her to the party. I do, and now I live in such a world."

(The quotation is an excerpt from remarks delivered at the Millennium March on Washington, April 30, 2000)

CONGRESSWOMAN TAMMY BALDWIN
Member of the United States House of Representatives
Representing the 3rd Congressional District of Wisconsin

DREAM

"DREAM LOFTY DREAMS, AND AS YOU DREAM
SO SHALL YOU BECOME." —James Allen

Young people today need to understand that they truly can find a way to live their particular dream if they creatively pursue that dream. So many children today are not encouraged to pursue excellence, but are satisfied with mediocrity.

PETER H. BABCOCK
Former Vice President/General Manager
The Atlanta Hawks
The National Basketball Association

DUTY

DO YOUR DUTY.

"It is no longer I who live, but it is Christ who lives in me. And the life I now live in the flesh, I live by faith in the Son of God, who loved me and gave himself for me." Galatians 2:20 is my favorite passage of scripture.

CHARLES (CHUCK) COLSON
White House Aide to President Richard Nixon
Founder of Prison Fellowship Ministries
Author

DYNAMITE

My team understands that "dynamite" means "excellence in action."

DON NEHLEN
Retired Head Football Coach, University of West Virginia

EARLY

NEVER MAKE A BAD DECISION EARLY.

Too often I have seen people in their personal and business lives not take the time to study and think things through, i.e., "do their homework," before making decisions that seriously influence their lives.

FRED W. HAISE JR.
Astronaut, *Apollo 13*

EDUCATION

EDUCATION, WORK, SELF-RESPECT, AND
PERSONAL RESPONSIBILITY

These are core values that I try to live by, and that I encourage
others to follow. I believe a path where one values and pursues
education, work, self-respect, and personal responsibility is a path
that puts dreams in reach and gives us the tools to change the
world for the better. By embracing these values, we all have the
opportunity to make the most of our lives, no matter how difficult
our circumstances or how great our challenges may be.

SHARON SAYLES BELTON
Former Mayor of Minneapolis, Minnesota

EFFORT

YOUR VERY BEST EFFORT EVERY TIME

Life is too short to cruise by—every time we have a chance to do something, it should be the "very best effort" possible!!

ROBERT C. WRIGHT
President and Chief Executive Officer
National Broadcasting Company, Inc.

EMBRACE

It evokes many attitudes and actions that suggest support, love, inclusion, thoughtfulness, commitment and others that reflect humanity in its most nurturing sense. If the challenge is to choose a word that says the most about the human condition as it should be, I think "embrace" does that.

BILL BOGAARD
Mayor of Pasadena, California

EMPATHY

KINDNESS AND EMPATHY

Kindness comes out of empathy. If you can feel what another is feeling—even if the other is an enemy—you will be kind to them. These two would stop all cruelty.

ALIX COREY
Actor on Broadway

EMPHASIZE

YOU GET WHAT YOU EMPHASIZE.

You focus and work hard at what you emphasize. Therefore you improve in that area.

BOB TOLEDO
Former Head Football Coach, UCLA

EMPOWER

As a mother and a reporter I have seen how a person can transform their lives and circumstances through empowerment. It's all about taking responsibility and taking action. Empowerment—a tremendous gift to give
or receive.

LEEZA GIBBONS
Television Talk Show Host, Author

EMPOWERMENT

EMPOWERED

To be empowered is to believe in oneself and possess the tools to act on that belief. I believe that empowerment, the recognition that each of us matters, that each of us can make a difference, one person at a time, or acting together in concert, not only provides a basis for a successful participatory democratic government, but gives us the inspiration and the will to think of ourselves as agents for the creation of a better world.

Empowerment fosters respect, for once we value ourselves, we have less inclination to devalue others. Empowerment leads us to social and personal happiness. Once empowered, we reach out to serve, help, and embrace others and that allows a state of spiritual wholeness. Ultimately, I believe, we're only here to serve and love each other.

PETER YARROW
Musician, Peter, Paul, and Mary

ENERGY

Energy plus talent, you're a king.
Energy but no talent, you're still a prince.
Talent but no energy, you're a pauper.

LORD JEFFREY ARCHER
Author
Former Member of the British Parliament

ENTHUSIASM

Its Greek root means "God in us."

KEN BURNS
Historian, Filmmaker

ENTHUSIASM

My definition (of enthusiasm) is the spiritual light inside radiating without. Each of us can cultivate enthusiasm and by so doing tune into and turn on everyone else to their full potential and the manifestation of their individual genius.

MARK V. HANSEN
Writer, Co-author of *Chicken Soup for the Soul*

ETHICS

Throughout my life and career, whenever I've been faced with choices ("do good," "be professional," "be moral," "do the right thing," etc.), this word "ethics" has epitomized the right thing for me to do (if **only** I had always listened to my own advice!!).

VICE ADMIRAL RICHARD H. TRULY
Astronaut, Pilot of the Space Shuttle *Columbia* on Mission STS-2
Commander of the Space Shuttle *Challenger* on Mission STS-8
Director of the National Renewable Energy Laboratory

EVIL

"AN EVIL DEED COMMITTED WILL FOLLOW THE
EVILDOER JUST LIKE A WHEEL FOLLOWS A HOOF
OF THE OX THAT BEARS THE YOKE."
—Lord Buddha

I believe this.

VIVENDRA LINTOTAWELA, F.C.A.
Chairman, John Keells Holdings
Sri Lanka

EXCEL

As a young man my mother suggested that one should not merely
just get by, but rather should be the best you can be, i.e., excel.

JAMES J. FLORIO
President and Chief Executive Officer, XSPAND
Former Governor of New Jersey

EXCELLENT

To excel is to live; to invigorate and be invigorated; to shine; to reach.

MARY MATALIN
Assistant to the President and Counselor to the Vice President
The United States Government
Author

EXCELLENT

"ALL THINGS EXCELLENT ARE AS DIFFICULT AS THEY ARE RARE."—Spinoza

It informs all my work as almost a mantra. As a film producer, each new project calls forth this challenge. It hangs as a motto in my offices. These words are shared with the entire crew, which inspires and stimulates a rich collaboration. And for my personal life, it helps to remind me to "keep on keepin' on."

MARIAN REES
Film Producer

EXPERIENCE

THERE IS NO SUBSTITUTE FOR EXPERIENCE.

This is an expression I find myself using quite often, in counseling family members, friends, and co-workers to get the best help they can to solve problems. This is not just another way of urging people to seek the advice of their elders, although that is often a good idea. Even young people can have a significant experience, which can be of benefit to others. It all depends on an individual's commitment to doing things wisely and well.

CORETTA SCOTT KING
Social Activist, Civil Rights Leader
Widow of Dr. Martin Luther King Jr.

FACTS

Facts are the building blocks of journalism, and journalism based solidly on facts is a building block of freedom.

PHILIP S. REVZIN
Vice President, International
Dow Jones and Company, Inc.

FAIR

BE FAIR.

This phrase embodies the principle I am most often urging my fellow public officials to adopt. I do so because I believe our private free market system does a superb job of creating wealth, but does less well in seeing that its benefits are made available fairly. The role of government in our society should be to provide a basic level of fairness for all people that we would otherwise not achieve. And I find also that as vague as that phrase seems to be, in most concrete situations people really do understand what fairness is, even if they are resistant to implementing it.

CONGRESSMAN BARNEY FRANK
Member of the United States House of Representatives
Representing the 4th District of Massachusetts

FAITH

My mother taught me that through faith all things you dream of are possible. In the darkest moments, faith even the size of a mustard seed can produce miracles.

Kim Morgan Greene
Actor

FAITH

Allows me to rise with the sun in the morning with a smile on my face and a smile in my heart.

Ron Silver
Movie Director, Primiparous Productions Inc.
Tony Award-Winning Actor
Activist, Founder of the Creative Coalition

FAMILY

This word should be treasured. Because without family, there would be no love whatsoever. I'm blessed to have a great family, without them I'd be lost.

BOBBY RYDELL
Rock and Roll Musician, Singer

FEAR

FEAR GOD WHEREVER YOU ARE, ERASE YOUR BAD DEEDS BY DOING GOOD DEEDS, DEAL WITH EVERYBODY IN A DECENT MANNER.

This is a saying of Prophet Muhammad (PBUH) which describes how human nature should be.

ABDULLAH O. NASSEEF
President, World Muslim Congress
Jeddah, Saudi Arabia

FEARLESS

We all have a right and a basic human need—to live without fear. Fear causes us to retreat, withdraw emotionally (and often physically) from community, to view strangers with suspicion. It leads to racism, sexism, homophobia, religious intolerance. It changes the way we live, rarely for the good.

DR. PETER RHINES
Professor of Oceanography, University of Washington

FIGHT

FOR ALL THESE THINGS I HAVE ONLY BEGUN TO FIGHT.

I would nominate Roosevelt's words at the height of the 1936 election. The GOP had challenged him as to whether he would continue with his New Deal reforms and this was Roosevelt's answer. I like it because it reflects his courage and conviction—qualities that are often notably absent from today's American politicians.

JAMES MACGREGOR BURNS
Presidential Historian
Author, Pulitzer Prize for Biographies on Roosevelt

81

FIGHT

FIGHT THE GOOD FIGHT.
FINISH THE RACE.
KEEP THE FAITH.

It is the old boxer and Marine's all too frequent admonishment to my children, a paraphrase from 2nd Timothy, with apologies to Paul. Semper Fidelis.

Lieutenant Colonel Oliver L. North
President and Founder of Freedom Alliance
Host of the Nationally Syndicated Program *War Stories*

FLEXIBLE

In business and life we must be prepared to react to change, most of which we have no control over. Therefore, we must retain a sense of humor as we remain flexible and adjust to whatever life brings.

DON LOGAN
Chairman, Media and Communications Group
AOL Time Warner

FOCUS

If you never lose sight—if you never waver—if you never go off track—if you always stay on target without any diversion, you always succeed at whatever goal you set for yourself or for others.

ROBIN LEACH
Television Personality
Lifestyles of the Rich and Famous

FOOTBALL

IT IS IMPORTANT TO PLAY THE GAME OF
FOOTBALL ONE PLAY AT A TIME.

Football is a series of explosive plays followed by a break in the
action. Ofttimes a player will save himself for the fourth quarter or
a key third down play. However, if he concentrates and focuses on
playing in the present and playing each play as hard as he possibly
can, he ofttimes avoids the pitfall of attempting to save himself
and pace himself throughout the game.

This attitude is important not just for football but for life
in general in that large tasks often look insurmountable when
looked at as a whole. However, when a task is broken down into
small manageable elements, it is possible to give maximum effort
in accomplishing the minute-by-minute or day-by-day portion
of the task, and eventually the whole project is accomplished.
It is very important to play "in the present" and perform "in the
present" as much as possible.

CONGRESSMAN TOM OSBORNE
United States House of Representatives from the 3rd
Congressional District of Nebraska
Former Head Football Coach, University of Nebraska

FORGIVENESS

Someone's always messin' up (usually me)
So someone's always in need of forgiveness.
"Father, forgive them for they know not what they do"—
That is the model we should try to follow.

LARRY GATLIN
Grammy Award-Winning Country Music Singer
Songwriter

FORGIVENESS

It's better to forgive than live your life with hate.

BIG TINY LITTLE
"Mr. Piano Personality" Entertainer

FORWARD

FORWARD IN THE STRUGGLE

This is a phrase from a speech my grandfather gave; it has guided my professional life.

JULIAN BOND
Chairman of the NAACP
Civil Rights Leader
Distinguished Scholar in Residence, American University
Faculty Member in the History Department, University of Virginia

FREE

THERE IS NO FREE LUNCH, AND, YOU GET OUT
WHAT YOU PUT IN.

I didn't create either of these but they rule my life. If the first one needs any explanation, it simply means that nobody ain't gonna do it **for** you. You have to do the struggling, striving, achieving yourself.

HELEN GURLEY BROWN
Editor-in-Chief, International Relations, *Cosmopolitan*

FREE

THERE IS NO FREE ICE CREAM.

In life, nothing comes easy and nothing is free.
If you want something, you have to work for it.

CLEM HASKINS
Former Head Coach, Men's Basketball
University of Minnesota

FREEDOM

DR. ANDREI ILLARIONOV
Advisor to the President of the Russian Federation
Russia

FREEDOM

It is the most powerful force in human history.

JEFF MACNELLY
Cartoonist

FREEDOM

FREEDOM IS WON BY ACCEPTING THE CUP AS OFFERED NOT ALTERED.

It has deep personal meaning to me as a reminder to reality.

MARTIN SHEEN
Actor, *The West Wing*

FREEDOM

I offer this particular word to you because I thought of it when I was four years old. In 1939, I wanted to know where freedom was, what it was. Twenty years later, I was reading a book by L. Ron Hubbard (*Dianetics: the Modern Science of Mental Health*) and saw that there was a way to freedom. That I could find my way through the labyrinth of ideas about freedom and understand it. That led me to Scientology—the study of knowing how to know. I know what freedom is.

REVEREND HEBER JENTZSCH
President of The Church of Scientology International

FREEDOM

FREEDOM AND RESPONSIBILITY

These two words are inseparable because there cannot be responsibility without freedom and vice versa freedom without responsibility might lead to chaos.

It is true that we are all born free. However, we are responsible exactly because we are free to choose better than worse solutions for our lives and the lives of other beings in our neighborhood.

Therefore, the balance between the freedom of choice and the responsibility for life is the key for our individual and global salvation.

His Excellence Dr. Mustafa Ceric
The Grand Mufti of Bosnia
Sarajevo, Bosnia-Herzegovina

FRIENDSHIP

ON FRIENDSHIP

At times when I am feeling low
I hear from a friend and then
my worries start to go away
and I am on the mend
No matter what the doctors say—
and their studies never end
the best cure of all, when spirits fall,
is a kind word from a friend.
—John Wooden

This phrase comes from the man I respect and love very deeply.
My coach—John Wooden.

DENNY CRUM
Former Head Coach, Men's Basketball
University of Louisville

FRUIT

The fruit of SILENCE is Prayer
The fruit of PRAYER is Faith
The fruit of FAITH is Love
The fruit of LOVE is Service
The fruit of SERVICE is PEACE

I have enclosed a card herewith an expression which I love to
repeat to everybody I meet. I gladly call it my Business Card.

MOTHER TERESA
Leader of the Order of Missionaries of Charity
Nobel Peace Laureate, 1979

FUSS

I AIN'T MAKING NO FUSS.

I use it frequently in response to the polite greeting of "How are you?" I heard it as a child on the lips of adult Negroes on the farm, and those people were awe-inspiring and filled me with wonder. It means, "I may not be all that important in the world's view, but I am well content." It resonates to the initiate of love of Jesus and tolerance of man, and is a much stronger reply than "just tolerable."

DR. FERROL A. SAMS JR.
Author, Physician

GENTLE

TO TAME THE SAVAGENESS OF MAN AND MAKE
GENTLE THE LIFE OF THIS WORLD.

Some twenty years ago, I read these words posted outside a candidate's storefront. They've stayed in my memory, as what we need in
every neighborhood, and what may be needed to save our civilization.

MARSHA HUNT
Actor

GIFTS

WHAT YOU ARE IS GOD'S GIFT TO YOU, WHAT YOU
BECOME IS YOUR GIFT TO GOD! TODAY I GAVE ALL I
HAVE, WHAT I'VE KEPT I'VE LOST FOREVER!

Two of my favorites.

LEON BARMORE
Louisiana Tech University, Former Head Coach, Women's Basketball
Member of the Women's Basketball Hall of Fame

GIGGLE

It's nearly impossible to giggle if you're feeling anger or sadness. I can think of no more pleasurable sound than a child's giggle. And if a cartoon of mine produces a giggle, then I consider it a success.

LARRY WRIGHT
Editorial Cartoonist
Detroit News

GIVE

You only have what you give.

ISABEL ALLENDE
Author

GLIDE

Olympic Figure Skater
Gold Medalist in 1988

GLOBAL

WE ARE ALL MEMBERS OF A GLOBAL COMMUNITY
WITH A SHARED DESTINY. "IMPROVING THE STATE OF
THE WORLD" REQUIRES A COMMITMENT FROM
EACH OF US TO CONTRIBUTE IN A POSITIVE WAY TO
BUILD.

PROFESSOR KLAUS SCHWAB
Founder and President, The World Economic Forum
Switzerland

GO

GO FOR BROKE.

That's the way I have always looked at golf and pretty much, life itself.

ARNOLD PALMER
Professional Golfer

GOAL

Bosnian Handicrafts set the goal seven years ago, and it keeps us moving forward to reach the goal in the time frame. Our vision is to create a manufacturing company that sells Bosnian handicrafts to major retailers throughout the world. The goal is to have annual sales of US $1,000,000 by 2005, have 1,000 women of Bosnia and Herzegovina supporting themselves and their families through craft production, and one floor in Saks Fifth Avenue selling our products.

LEJLA RADONCIC
Chief Executive Director, Bosnian Handicrafts
Bosnia and Herzegovina

GOAL

YOU WILL REACH YOUR GOAL IF YOU TRY
HARD ENOUGH.

Keep the faith—and think positive.

ANDREW V. MCLAGLEN
Movie Director

GOD

GOD LOVES ME UNCONDITIONALLY.

That makes me a VSP, a very special person.
This uplifts me because it tells me that my worth is infinite. I
don't have to impress God or anybody else. God loves me, period,
and everything flows from that.

ARCHBISHOP DESMOND M. TUTU
Archbishop Emeritus, South Africa
Nobel Peace Laureate, 1984

GOD

GOD FIRST, FAMILY SECOND, THIRD TAKE ACTION
AND MOTIVATION WILL FOLLOW.

I live this way. God has been my audience and friend. My family is
very important to me. I believe in following your goals—your
dreams. Most of all I believe in hard work—action—team work.

CANDACE AZZARA
Actor

GOD

GOD IS A GOOD GOD!

That one statement revolutionized my life and launched my ministry.

In 1947 I was a young pastor and university student. One
morning I was about to catch the bus to school when I remembered
that I hadn't read the Bible, as was my custom. I ran back home,
picked up my Bible, and it fell open to the little book of III John.
What I read that morning changed my life—abruptly and completely. The second verse says, "Beloved, I wish above all things that
thou mayest prosper and be in health, even as thy soul prospereth."
I'd read the Bible through a hundred times and had never seen that

verse. Immediately coming up out of my being was the realization that God is a good God. Up until then I'd struggled with what people—even ministers had taught about God. When I was only seventeen, I was stricken with tuberculosis in both lungs. As I lay hovering between life and death, religious people came to visit me, and they told me to be patient, to accept my affliction, for it was God's will. One minister told me, "Son, God has put this on you." Yet those same people wanted me to get saved! It was a paradox; here God was afflicting me yet wanting me to love Him. Something inside me said it wasn't true.

That's when God touched my life! He saved my soul, healed me from tuberculosis, loosed my stuttering tongue, and called me into the healing ministry! The day I learned that God loves me and wants me to be in health and prosper, I began to see Him as a good God—a God who knows our names and is closer to us than our breath. I began to see that God did not come to afflict people but to heal them, not to beat them down but lift them up, not to destroy them but to save them. John 10:10 says, "the thief cometh not, but for to steal, and to kill and to destroy. I am come that they might have life, and that they might have it more abundantly."

God is a good God who wants to bless His people, heal them, and do those miracles for them that no one else can. Oh, how I wish I could shout it from the rooftops: "GOD IS A GOOD GOD!"

ORAL ROBERTS
Television Evangelist
Founder and First President of Oral Roberts University

GOD

GOD IS JUSTICE.

And we who are in the image of God must be about justice also.
Out of love.

REV. PHILIP BERRIGAN
Priest, Author, Social Activist

GOD

GOD NEVER SHUTS ONE DOOR BUT HE
OPENS ANOTHER.

Irish proverb. Leave it in God's hands and He always finds a way.
Keep the faith.

ROBERT J. (BOBBY) ROSS
Former Head Coach in the National Football League
Detroit Lions and San Diego Chargers

GOD

GOD WILLING

It is an everyday phrase we use to acknowledge the Lord's importance, the Lord's approval as utterly significant for us, during our time spent here.

DR. ROBERT COLES
Child Psychiatrist
James Agee Professor of Social Ethics at Harvard University
Author, 1973 Pulitzer Prize Winner for *Children of Crisis* (5 volumes)

GOD

IF GOD BE FOR ME, WHO CAN BE AGAINST ME?
(quote from the Bible)

Because it says it all.

CHARLIE DANIELS
Country Music Singer, *The Charlie Daniels Band*

GOD

GOD LOVES US EXACTLY AS WE ARE, BUT GOD
LOVES US TOO MUCH TO LEAVE US THERE.

REVEREND DOCTOR WILLIAM SLOANE COFFIN
Former Senior Minister of the Riverside Church of New York City
Author

GOD

GOD HAS BEEN VERY GOOD TO ME.

KIRK DOUGLAS
Actor

GOOD

"AND GOD SAW EVERYTHING THAT HE HAD MADE,
AND, BEHOLD, IT WAS VERY GOOD."
—Genesis 1:31

RAY CONIFF
Musical Conductor, Composer

GOOD

"LET US NOT GROW WEARY IN DOING GOOD
FOR IN DUE SEASON WE SHALL REAP IF WE DO
NOT LOSE HEART."
—Galatians 6:9

It has helped to sustain me in hard times, to remind me of an obligation to press on through frustration, sadness, and losses.

WILLIAM JEFFERSON CLINTON
Forty-Second President of the United States

GRACE

Without it, our human striving, whether painful or easy, triumphant or disastrous, has no meaning.

STEPHEN L. CARTER
William Nelson Cromwell Professor of Law, Yale University
Author

GRACE

The word *grace* embodies so many words for me. Grace is gentility, kindness and compassion. It is simplicity, humility and generosity. Grace expresses an attitude of gratitude, surrender and love. For me grace is the essence of feminine energy and the strength and dignity of the masculine. Grace is about the Divine in all of us. It is the beauty of all the blessings we have. Grace is for me a context of a way to honor integrity, service and peace. Thoughts of grace open my heart and give me faith in something outside of myself.

JUDITH LIGHT
Actor

GRACE

It means to me—"courage under fire"
"cutting your fellow man and woman
some slack"
"the offering of consideration, comfort
and love"
"a state of being—a feeling of
contentment."

JOHN S. PALMER
National Correspondent
NBC News

GRACE

AMAZING: GRACE.

I bless you with my favorite word, *grace*. Perhaps the gentlest of
words in the English language, "grace" touches all who seek the
true meaning of life.

JOHN MACK CARTER
President of the Hearst Corporation
Hearst Newspapers

GRACE

When I imagine the deep wounds of the people of Rwanda and yet I do not see them crazy people, I realize it is by the grace of God that our people endure.

I think the people of Rwanda would be angry, against the church as thousands of them were killed inside the church buildings while the church leadership kept silent, yet people go to church (as the people do not hold the church responsible for their suffering).

THE MOST REVEREND EMMANUEL M. KOLINI
Archbishop of the Province of the Episcopal Church
Bishop of the Episcopal Church of Rwanda/Diocese of Kigali
Rwanda

GRATITUDE

The older I am, the more grateful I become for the gifts of my life and relationships, the beauty of the world, and the hope and love God's grace gives each of us. Therefore, my favorite word is "gratitude." My favorite phrase, found in Henri Nouwen's powerful work, *The Return of the Prodigal Son,* is "the discipline of gratitude" which I try to practice every day.

SENATOR HILLARY RODHAM CLINTON
United States Senator from New York
Former First Lady of the United States

GRATITUDE

Life is beautiful when you entertain this world *constantly!* I know—because I'm *doing it!*

DORIS DAY
Actor

GRATITUDE

Spiritual health, mental health—even physical health and happiness start with being thankful.

An attitude of appreciation causes a person to see good in people, places, and circumstances.

Giving thanks never goes out of style.

CARL ERSKINE
Retired Major League Baseball Player
Brooklyn Dodgers

GROWTH

A STRONG COMMITMENT TO SUSTAINABLE GROWTH

Sustainable growth is not only an economic value but a social value. Economic growth distributed fairly—not one limited to just one part of the world—is one of the most effective weapons we have to build peace and to isolate and defeat our enemies.

CORRADO PASSERA
Chief Executive Officer
IntesaBci Group, Italy

GUIDELINES

BE ON TIME (OR TEN MINUTES EARLY).
GO TO CLASS EVERY DAY!
TRY YOUR BEST.

I give you these team guidelines so you will care about your job, get an education and, if you try your best, you won't fail!

GENE KEADY
Head Coach, Men's Basketball
Purdue University

GUMPTION

Gumption was my mother's word and, for her, it was part of "up by your own boot straps," combined with sticking by your word. People with gumption are the glue that keeps society together. Paradoxically, they're also the engine pulling society forward. Gumption is what we need a lot more of today.

HARRIET MILLER
Former Mayor of Santa Barbara, California

GURRIER

It is an old Dublin slang word that describes a low-life person or lout, but the word is only ever used with a degree (small) of affection—in the final analysis, it is never really nasty.

LOCHLANN QUINN
Chairman, Allied Irish Banks
Ireland

HAPPINESS

HAPPINESS & LOVE

This, I have been signing for autographs for forty years—to man, woman, or child; I truly wished it to them!

LEE MAJORS
Actor

HAPPY

EVERYBODY'S HAPPY AND THE GOOSE HANGS HIGH.

My father used to say it. He was from rural Louisiana (b. 1904). I don't really know the derivation, but it reminds me of happy times.

ALFRED UHRY
Playwright, *Driving Miss Daisy*

HEAR

IF YOU CAN'T HEAR IT, YOU CAN'T FEEL IT.

I have been a member of the music business for the past fifty years. I have worked with the Greats of Country Music, such as Hank Williams, Sr. and Elvis, Johnny Cash, and etc....In the past, the rule of thumb on making recordings has been, if the lyrics of the song are covered up by the background vocals or instruments, the record doesn't have a chance. Because, if the listeners can't hear it, they can't feel it! However with the advent of modern technology and increased power of amplification, the youth of America yells, "Turn it up! Turn it up!" Their reason is "If you can't hear it, you can't feel it."

I wish I had said, "Time changes everything."

MERLE KILGORE
Songwriter, Musician

HEART

It takes a big heart to work for the greater good.
It takes a strong heart to stand by your convictions, exercise leadership and do what's right, if not popular.
It takes an open heart to understand and accept other viewpoints.
It takes a kind heart to give someone the benefit of the doubt.

SENATOR BILL FRIST
United States Senator from Tennessee
Majority Leader of the Senate
Heart and Lung Transplant Surgeon

HEART

A RECTIFIED HEART

The ancient Chinese philosopher, Mencius, observed:
The men of old, wishing to clarify and diffuse throughout the
empire that light which comes from looking straight into the heart
and acting, first set up good government in their own states.
Desiring good government in their own states, they first organized
their families. Eager to organize their families, they first disciplined
themselves. And determined to discipline themselves,
they first rectified their hearts.

SIDNEY HARMAN
Executive Chairman, Harman International Industries

HIT

A HIT SONG DON'T CARE WHO WROTE IT.

Who knows where the hit really comes from and what makes it so?

JODY MILLER
Singer

"HOLY COW" & HUCKLEBERRY

They are two words that can be used for just about any situation—i.e., amazement, watching a great artist, seeing a good movie. Calling someone a "Huckleberry" is more a term of endearment, etc. Neither word offends or is in bad taste.

PHIL RIZZUTO
Hall of Fame Baseball Player
"The Scooter"
New York Yankees

HOLY JUMPING TOLEDO

I say it.

CARMEN BASILIO
Boxer
Member, International Boxing Hall of Fame

HOME

It conveys something of my dearest memories and holiest hopes, and something too of the most precious gifts I was ever given or was ever able to give. And because it reminds me of what I have spent my life looking for.

FREDERICK BUECHNER
Author

HOME

Home is my favorite word because for me it evokes a variety of feelings—shelter, work, love, and loss.

DONALD "SKIP" HAYS
Author

HOME

The place where you know you belong—where you don't have to explain yourself. A magnificent mother gave me a sense of that word.

ATHOL FUGARD
South African Playwright
Sorrows and Rejoicings

HONOR

Honor defines what public service should be about. It defines, for me, our all-volunteer military. It sets a standard that Presidents and all others, too, should use as their standard for service to our great country.

GEORGE H. W. BUSH
Forty-First President of the United States

HONOR

Without it one cannot exist.
It is a noble word that is about truth.

JIM NANTZ
Sportscaster, CBS-TV

HONOR

Today it is more "honored" in the breach than the observance.

EFREM ZIMBALIST JR.
Actor

HOPE

Without hope, can you live?

PETER HUGO ROELANT
Chef, Four Oaks
Bel Air, California

HOPE

Without hope there is no desire, without desire there is no expectation, without expectation there is no possibility of achievement or success. Nothing changes for the better in this world without someone hoping for it. The most important thing about hope—is having it.

LEO F. BUSCAGLIA
Author

HOPE

Without hope, the spirit fades. Hope rooted in a spiritual quest makes one strive to be better, to rise above daily challenges. Hope provides the fuel for transformation.

ELIZABETH BIRCH
Executive Director, The Human Rights Campaign

HOPE

Hope is central to peace of mind and to meeting challenges.

GERRY ADAMS
Leader of the Sinn Fein Party in Ireland

HOPE

Without hope, nothing is possible.

LOUETTA J. ROSS
Founder, Executive Director
Center for Human Rights Education

HOPE

It is the beacon that lights our path to the future.

SIDNEY SHELDON
Author

HOPE

Every positive change that has occurred on this planet is the result of individuals who had "hope" for mankind. No great deed was ever accomplished unless some individual had "hope" that the lot of man could be bettered.

ANNE ARCHER
Actor, Academy Award Nominee for her performance in
Fatal Attraction

HOPE

What else do we have?
I composed a mass "To Hope!" in which the priest sings "I wait in joyful hope for the coming of the Saviour, Jesus Christ."

DAVE BRUBECK
Musician, Jazz Pianist, Composer

HOW

HOW THE COW ATE THE CABBAGE PRETTY QUICK.

Relatives down in West Texas used this expression two, maybe three, generations ago! Use it however you like!

PAULA PRENTISS
Actor

HUGS

My simple message is "Everyone loves a hug!"

JACK MITCHELL
Clothier, Richards in Greenwich, Connecticut
Author of *Hug Your Customers*

HUMANITY

Humanity springs from us, comes from our past, is the one
assurance of our future, achieves all things, transcends all faiths
and all nationalities. But we have to learn to exercise humanity
collectively and not just individually, for only then will we be at
peace in our world.

SIR JOHN SULSTON
Director of the Human Genome Project in the United Kingdom
2002 Nobel Laureate for Physiology or Medicine

HUMANITY

HUMANITY AND HUMAN DIGNITY

During these troubled days when anger and self-righteousness rule, spurred by overwhelming military capability, one wonders where humility has gone. What justification is there to kill women, children, old people, to bomb universities, markets and hospitals? What is the meaning of life, of freedom, if one is denied basic human dignity? Can there be human dignity for a nation that has to bend its knees and call others masters?

DR. DEWI FORTUNA ANWAR
Director, Programme and Research
The Habibie Center, Indonesia

HUMILITY

In my work, I see people who survive in the most awful circumstances. They are often resourceful, resilient, and good-humoured.
We must never think we know better than they do how to run their
lives.

BARBARA STOCKING
Executive Director, Oxfam
Great Britain

HUMILITY

The key to being a successful leader is to recognize that many minds are better than one. An effective leader should therefore not be overly impressed with his or her own "good ideas." Arrogance is dangerous.

I believe that it is crucial to be completely open to the ideas and suggestions of others, if one is to take optimal advantage of opportunities or find the best solutions to problems. Humility is therefore an essential trait. Those lacking this trait will make mistakes that are created by their inability to honestly solicit and consider different viewpoints, as required to make the best decisions.

BRUCE ALBERTS
President, National Academy of Sciences

HUSTLE

Always keep moving, going forward, with basketball and life.

JIM CALHOUN
Head Coach, Men's Basketball
University of Connecticut

HYACINTHS

(My word) is based on a verse by James Terry White and is from his poem, "Not by Bread Alone."

"IF THOU OF FORTUNE BE BEREFT
AND IN THY STORE THERE BE BUT LEFT
TWO LOAVES, SELL ONE AND WITH THE DOLE
BUY HYACINTHS TO FEED THY SOUL."

I offer this particular word because it represents both the rebirth of spring and hope. One Valentine's Day, my children came home from school and found a flower pot swathed in green tissue on the kitchen table. As I unwrapped it, I recited the poem. The children laughed. They thought it was silly.

Several years later, on Valentine's Day following the death of their father, the florist delivered another plant swathed in green tissue. Hyacinths! They were from my children, with a card, "Hyacinths to feed thy soul."

INA R. FRIEDMAN
Author and Storyteller, *Escape or Die; True Stories of Young People Who Survived the Holocaust*

I

"I AM THE ALPHA AND THE OMEGA, THE BEGINNING AND THE END, THE FIRST AND THE LAST."
—Revelation 22:13

Christ is the Alpha and the Omega of my life. He is my everything; my constant joy and my daily inspiration.

HIS EMINENCE ARCHBISHOP DEMETRIOS
Primate of the Greek Orthodox Church America
Chairman of the Holy Eparchial Synod of Bishops

ICHIGO

ICHIGO (ONE CHANCE) ICHIE (ONE MEETING)
Japanese Phrase Meaning:
ONCE IN A LIFETIME MEETING
VALUE AND CHERISH THAT ONCE IN A LIFETIME
MEETING AS YOU MAY NEVER HAVE THE
OPPORTUNITY OF MEETING AGAIN.

As a chef, I've learned that every time I create a dish to be sent to a guest, that dish is meeting the guest for the very first time. Since Chaya Brasserie is an upscale dining establishment, many of the guests choose a special occasion to come and celebrate there, whether it be a birthday, anniversary, a first date, an engagement, etc. Since they are not usually your "regular/repeating" customers, whatever menu they choose, they must be "right" or their dining experience *and* the special occasion are both ruined. See, when something is not up to par with a dish one evening, *if* it's a repeating customer, he/she may have a understanding that perhaps the kitchen has missed a beat that time. They know what the dish is *supposed* to look/taste like. However, if it happened to a first time customer, h/she may never wish to come back again, just from one bad dish or experience.

SHIGEFUMI TACHIBE
Owner/Executive Chef, Chaya
Los Angeles, California

IDEALS

STEVE ALLEN
Television Personality

IF

JEAN KENNEDY SMITH
Former Ambassador to Ireland
Sister of President John F. Kennedy

IMAGINATION

It is the key to divine and human creation—we have to imagine what God has imagined. It gives us an idea of other worlds and the feelings of this one.

VICTOR HERNANDEZ CRUZ
Puerto Rican Poet, Novelist, Teacher

IMAGINE

I imagine that would be self-explanatory to most people.

TOM T. HALL
Grammy Award-Winning Musician,
Songwriter, Entertainer, Novelist

IMMORTALITY

It is the meaning of our existence to leave behind what we were put here on earth to do—so that others may learn and evolve from our fortunes and misfortunes. I am here to paint, inspire, and provoke. But, most of all, I am here to teach and learn from you. My paintings are my immortality; what is your immortality? *Carpe Diem.*

JOSEPH R. HANSON
Artist

IMPORTANT

"THERE IS NOTHING WRONG WITH BEING THE MOST
IMPORTANT PERSON UNDER THE SUN IF EVERYBODY
ELSE IS JUST AS IMPORTANT AS YOU ARE."
—L. Ron Hubbard

I like this quote because it explains to me the difference between
the words *important* and *valuable,* i.e., if a plane is crashing,
everybody on it is equally important, but the pilot flying the plane
is more valuable at that moment.

JOHN TRAVOLTA
Academy Award-Winning Actor

INEFFABLE

It is flexible and pertains to the inexpressible.

WILLIE MORRIS
Author, Journalist

INEQUALITY INSURANCE

I used the term "inequality insurance" in my latest book *The New Financial Order* to refer to a program to insure our society against the risk of worsening inequality. I argue there that there is a real risk that the trend over recent decades towards increasing economic inequality in our society may continue for decades more, leaving our society much more unequal in the future than it is today. In 1970, the bottom 40% of American families earned 18% of the income; by 1988 the bottom 40% of families earned only 14% of the income. Thirty years from now, it is entirely possible that the bottom 40% of American families will earn well under 10% of the income. Such an outcome would breed resentment and social unrest. This increased inequality could happen because computers continue to replace jobs, because poor people in foreign countries replace jobs here, or for other reasons. If inequality gets much worse, it will probably not be because some people got lazy and decided not to work, it is probably because of intrinsic changes in the economy. It is important to deal with the potential problem of increasing inequality before it happens, by putting in place a government program, like social security, that protects society against such an outcome.

DR. ROBERT JAMES SHILLER
Professor of Economics, Yale University

INFINITE

THE TRUE INFINITE

Borrowed from Hegel, this phrase succinctly registers the conviction that every dualism is in the end untenable both in theory and in practice—that, for example, to construe as and to live as if "body" and "spirit" are unalterably opposed is a less adequate positive than to affirm "embodied spirit."

DR. GEORGE RUPP
President and Chief Executive Officer
International Rescue Committee
Former President of Columbia University

INNER LIGHT

NOURISH YOUR INNER LIGHT THEN
TRUST IT TO ILLUMINATE YOUR PATH.

The phrase came from my father who, like me, believed in the
Quaker notion of "inner light."

BERNARD RANDS
Musician, Composer
Pulitzer Prize Winner for *Canti del Sole*, 1984
Grammy Award Winner for *Canti D'Amor*, 2000
Walter Bigelow Professor of Music, Harvard University

INNOVATION

STEVEN J. HEYER
President and Chief Operating Officer
The Coca-Cola Company

INNOVATION, INTEGRITY, EXCELLENCE, PREEMINENT

I have instituted four words in the organizations that I head to set a standard. The first three are innovation, integrity, excellence. The fourth gives us something to aspire to—preeminent.

PAT ROBERTSON
Chairman of the Board, Chief Executive Officer
The Christian Broadcasting Network, Inc.
Former President of the Christian Coalition

INSIGHT

1) Self-awareness is one key to happiness.
2) It's not the facts which matter, rather it's their meaning.
3) Smart is the ability to bring experience to a new situation.
4) Understanding the needs and motivations of others is necessary for achievement.

Without insight, you must rely on denial to cope with life's twists and turns.

NEIL S. BRAUN
President, Media, Vast Video
Former President of NBC Television

INSTANT

WE LIVE BUT FOR AN INSTANT IN ETERNITY AND
THE ONLY THING THAT MATTERS IS WHAT WE DO
WITH THAT INSTANT. THAT IS THE ONLY LEGACY
WE LEAVE.

It (this particular phrase) means a great deal to me.

SENATOR DIANNE FEINSTEIN
United States Senator from California
Former Mayor of San Francisco

INTEGRITY

When my son was thirteen, I gave him an engraved pistol—with
one word, "INTEGRITY."
—My Phrase—
No man left my presence who wasn't a little wiser and a little
richer.

BUDDY HACKETT
Comedian

INTEGRITY

A precious gift from my father that I hope I can live up to.

ADI IGNATIUS
Executive Editor, Time, Inc.

INTEGRITY

Without this quality, nothing is possible—no law, no order, no civility, no decency—is crucial.

ROBERT L. DILENSCHNEIDER
Founder and Principal of The Dilenschneider Group
Author

INTEGRITY

UNWAVERING INTEGRITY

It's the only way—and the easiest way—to live life.

ROBERT A. ECKERT
Chairman and Chief Executive Officer
Mattel, Inc.

INTEGRITY

I believe integrity is an internal character value against which
I must always measure my actions.

ADMIRAL BOBBY R. INMAN
United States Navy, Retired

INTEGRITY

Of character and intellect.

PETER R. KANN
Publisher, *The Wall Street Journal*

INTEGRITY

All you have is your integrity.

DENNIS NALLY
Chairman and Senior Partner
PricewaterhouseCoopers

INTELLECTUAL

I AM AN INTELLECTUAL PESSIMIST AND
AN EMOTIONAL OPTIMIST.

I think (this phrase) expresses the right stance to live by—be aware
of the risks, but act as if things will come out all right.

LESTER THUROW
Lemelson Professor of Management and Economics
Massachusetts Institute of Technology

INTENSITY

SUSTAINED INTENSITY

KENNETH D. LEWIS
Chairman and Chief Executive Officer
Bank of America

IRREVERENCE

It is a word I have always used to describe America. It is what has made people from the bottom up feel that they can defy the conventional wisdom in all walks of life to accomplish what they think is right.

MORTIMER B. ZUCKERMAN
Chairman and Editor-in-Chief, *U.S. News & World Report*

JANUS

Janus was the Roman god with two faces—one is the light, one is the shade.
　　To me he represents the challenge of globalization. The face in the shade reflects a world in which the rich get richer and the poor, poorer. The face in the light reflects a world in which everyone is better off.

GORDON CONWAY
President of the Rockefeller Foundation

JESUS CHRIST

No other person who has ever lived has impacted the world in a greater way. Schools, universities, and hospitals have been built in His Name. Lives have been changed because of the faith, hope, and love they have found in the "King of Kings and Lord of Lords." Even our calendar is based on His life (this is 2003 A.D. in the year of our Lord). The Bible describes Him as the God-man. I believe that through His sacrifice on the cross that He is the only way to heaven and eternal life.

GARY VARVEL
Editorial Cartoonist, *The Indianapolis Star-News*

JEWISH

A JEWISH RENAISSANCE

To insure the continuing of the Jewish people, we need a renaissance or rebirth of our religion. Too many generations are Jewishly ignorant. We must attempt to teach our young pride in their Judaism. That necessitates knowledge.

EDGAR M. BRONFMAN
Former Chairman, the Seagram Company Ltd.
President of the World Jewish Congress and the
World Jewish Reconstruction Organization

JOY

THE word is JOY! That's what gets me through the day and I can share that word with anyone I meet. JOY Always.

THE LADY CHABLIS, THE DOLL
Entertainer in Savannah, Georgia
Made famous by the novel *Midnight in the Garden of Good and Evil*

JOY / DESPAIR

Joy is a positive commandment; Despair a negative one.
These two words have been especially meaningful to me of late.
The early nineteenth century Hassidic rebbe, Nachman of Brezlov,
said: "Always remember: joy is not merely incidental to your
spiritual quest. It is vital." Incidentally, it was he who also told
his disciples: "Never despair! Never! It is forbidden to give up
hope." To embrace joy and reject despair are not options
(among other feelings one might choose) in the spiritual life;
they are commands. That makes everything easier, of course,
but more demanding than ever in the exercise of faith.

DR. BELDEN C. LANE
Author, Distinguished Professor in the Humanities
Saint Louis University

JUDGE

JUDGE NOT

Nothing has so poisoned our public life as the audacity with which we judge the motives of others.

JACK W. GERMOND
Political Columnist
Author, *Fat Man in a Middle Seat: Forty Years of Covering Politics*
Regular Panelist on *Inside Washington*

JUDGMENT

GOOD JUDGMENT

The key to both success and happiness.

THEODORE C. SORENSEN
Special Counsel to President John F. Kennedy
Lawyer with Paul, Weiss, Rifkind, Wharton & Garrison

JUSTICE

Justice, like beauty, is in the mind of the beholder. It's the cornerstone of our system of law based on liberty.

ROBERT F. SHAPIRO
Attorney

JUSTICE

I believe the words of the prophet Micah, chapter 6, verse 8, that the request of the Lord to do justice, to love kindness, and to walk humbly with our God, are the center of the Judeo/Christian faith. It is the prophetic mandate that propels my life and ministry.

THE RIGHT REVEREND JANE HOLMES DIXON
Suffragan Bishop, Washington Diocese of the Episcopal Church
(Retired)

KIND

BE KIND TO ALL YOU MEET.

Kindness is a wonderful gift we can both receive and give.

MAIREAD MAGUIRE
Nobel Peace Laureate, 1976
Northern Ireland

KINDNESS

At moments along the path my life has taken there have been acts of kindness which helped me survive and go on hoping for the best.

HAL HOLBROOK
Actor

KINDNESS

Because it softens the bumps in life!

CELESTE HOLM
Actor

KINDNESS AND COMPASSION

Someone once asked me what words would I like written about me after my death—in addition to the standard verbage such as beloved son, compassionate father, loving husband, and I responded "as a kind and compassionate person who cared for and helped others."

MICHAEL GOLDSTEIN
Former Chief Executive Officer
Toys "R" Us, Inc.

KNOW

I DON'T KNOW.

Scientists, in general, do not use this phrase often enough.

DR. EDWARD TELLER
Physicist, Author
Senior Research Fellow at the Hoover Institution on War,
Revolution and Peace, Stanford University

LAUGH

IT IS EASY TO LAUGH BUT IT IS NOT EASY TO
MAKE PEOPLE LAUGH.

I'll give you a phrase which has been an experience as far as my
work as an editorial cartoonist and a humourist is concerned.
This phrase has made me appreciate my work even more and,
in many times, acted as a challenge and my driving force.

GADO

Editorial Cartoonist, *The Daily Nation*, Kenya

LAUGH

Laughter is infectious, and is a tonic which can cure most ills.

LEONARD A. LAUDER
Chairman, Estée Lauder Company

LAUGHTER

As somebody said in a novel I wrote, "Laughter is the only thing that cuts trouble down to a size where you can talk to it."

DAN JENKINS
Author

LEAD

"WITH A GOOD CONSCIENCE OUR ONLY SURE
REWARD, WITH HISTORY THE FINAL JUDGE OF OUR
DEEDS, LET US GO FORTH TO LEAD THE LAND WE
LOVE, ASKING HIS BLESSING AND HIS HELP, BUT
KNOWING THAT HERE ON EARTH GOD'S WORK MUST
TRULY BE OUR OWN."
—John F. Kennedy (Inaugural Address, January 20, 1961)

TIMOTHY RUSSERT
Television Journalist
Senior Vice President and Washington Bureau Chief of NBC News
Moderator of *Meet the Press*

LEADERSHIP

At some point, each of us will find ourselves in a position to assume leadership in one form or another. Our responsibility as individuals is to be prepared for that moment by following our conscience and doing what's right. You never know who's looking to you for an example.

SENATOR FRED THOMPSON
Former United States Senator from Tennessee
Actor

LEADERSHIP

Leadership is the result of the study, determination, and strength of each day. We must learn to live alone. The energy of these convictions must pass through the test of misfortune.

It is in our imagination that we have cherished a dream of peace and living together (in harmony). Navigating in reality, and guided by the common idea of the Mountain (religious reference), we are disposed to achieve this dream.

Our reciprocity is to work in order that in the century that comes, in our land exists more warmth in the home and less crying, more bread and less scars, more tolerance with the diversity and zero tolerance for crime, more authority and less power, more liberty and less fear, more solidarity and less individual ambition, a purer soul, a warmer character, beliefs in collective dignity (human dignity), more global justice and less globalization...and zero violence. We work for a greater sense of region (regional pride) and of autonomy, and a greater responsibility on the part of the country, Colombia.

THE HONORABLE ALVARO URIBE VELEZ
President of Colombia

154

LEVITY

LEVITY IS THE LUBRICANT OF CRISIS.

Humor can solve most difficult confrontations.

WALLY SCHIRRA
Astronaut, Command Pilot on *Apollo 7*

LIBERTY

Liberty is the people's most precious possession, and the most difficult and elusive to acquire and maintain.

NORMAN DORSEN
Frederick I. and Grace A. Professor of Law
Co-director of Arthur Garfield Civil Liberties Program
New York University School of Law
Activist on Issues of Human Rights and Civil Liberties

LIE

DON'T LIE.

There's only one way to get out of a lie: tell another.

BILLY HARDWICK
Professional Bowler

LIFE

CHOOSE LIFE!

It's always our basic choice: what leads to life and its enhancement
or its diminishment.

SISTER HELEN PREJEAN
Nun, Sisters of St. Joseph of Medaille
Author of *Dead Man Walking*

LIFE

LIFE IS THE SHOWING FORTH OF THE VERY
SELF OF GOD.

A phrase from the *Daily Word*. It's just a nice way to get
a mind-set for the coming day.

JANET LEIGH
Actor

LIFE

One starts to live when you can live outside of yourself.
Life is a gift and we must contribute in return—when we fail
to do so, we fail to adequately answer why we are here.

MIKE MEDAVOY
Chairman and Chief Executive Officer, Phoenix Pictures, Inc.
Academy Award Winner

LIFE

I have a word for you. It is "Life." Some people live without a life. My Ministry is about Possibility Living.

THE REVEREND DR. ROBERT A. SCHULLER
Vice President of the Crystal Cathedral Ministries
Television Minister on *Hour of Power*
Author

LIFE

SURE, I'M SCARED, BUT SOMEBODY'S GOT TO DO IT!
OR TAKE WHAT YOU WANT OUT OF LIFE,
BUT PAY FOR IT.

ROGER WILLIAMS
Concert Pianist

LIMB

DON'T BE AFRAID TO GO OUT ON A LIMB.
THAT'S WHERE THE FRUIT IS!

A person must take some risks in life if he wants to "do his thing" differently and better than others in his profession.

STEVE SPURRIER
Head Football Coach, Washington Redskins
The National Football League

LISTEN

I'm selecting this word because to communicate well means to be a good listener, to bridge differences means to be a good listener, and to form genuine partnerships means to understand and listen to all parties' concerns. So, from my perspective, especially today when the world seems so divided, and passionately so at times, listening takes on a new importance.

KATHY BLOOMGARDEN
Chief Executive Officer, Ruder Finn, Inc.

LISTEN

You can hear more that way.

MARGRET EDSON
School teacher
Pulitzer Prize-Winning Playwright, *Wit*

LIVE

IT'S NOT HOW LONG YOU LIVE BUT HOW YOU
LIVE YOUR LIFE THAT COUNTS.

Our purpose is to live not simply exist!

COLONEL R. WALTER CUNNINGHAM
Astronaut, *Apollo 7*
Managing General Partner, The Genesis Fund

LIVE

IF YOU WANT TO MAKE IT, YOU CAN'T FAKE IT...
YOU GOTTA LIVE IT!

It's self-explanatory.

HANK WILLIAMS JR.
Country Music Singer, Grammy Winner in 1987
First Country Music Singer to Win an Emmy

LOOK

DON'T LOOK BACK IN ANGER.
DON'T LOOK FORWARD IN FEAR.
LOOK AROUND IN AWARENESS.

We cannot change the past. We can't predict the future.
But we can enjoy today with optimism for the future.

JENNY CRAIG
Weight Management Expert

LORD

"TRUST IN THE LORD WITH ALL YOUR HEART,
AND LEAN NOT ON YOUR OWN UNDERSTANDING,
IN ALL YOUR WAYS ACKNOWLEDGE HIM AND
HE WILL MAKE YOUR PATHS STRAIGHT."
—Proverbs 3: 5-6 NIV

These verses contain some great promises from God.
I want my life to count for God so I try to do all it says.

CHARLES DUKE
Astronaut, *Apollo 16*

LORD

LORD, SUPPORT US ALL THE DAY LONG OF THIS
TROUBLED LIFE, UNTIL THE SHADOWS LENGTHEN
AND THE EVENING COMES AND THE BUSY WORLD IS
HUSHED, THE FEVER OF LIFE IS OVER, AND OUR
WORK IS DONE. THEN, LORD, IN YOUR MERCY,
GRANT US A SAFE LODGING AND A HOLY REST, AND
PEACE AT THE LAST; THROUGH JESUS CHRIST OUR
LORD, AMEN.

My favorite would be this prayer by John Newman; someone says
it's the most beautiful sentence in the English language.

MARTIN E. MARTY
Author, Professor, Church Historian
Regularly named one of the most influential
Religious Figures in the United States

LOVE

We will never think our way into heaven. Only love will guide us.
Our history must inform us. My mother's maiden name was
"Love." She is now long dead. But African Americans know that
we live as the product not only of violence (real as that was and is)
but also the product of love. Perhaps love will show us the way.

REVEREND WILLIAM G. SINKFORD
President of the Unitarian Universalist Association

LOVE

THE FIRST CHANCE YOU GET, DO SOMETHING NICE FOR SOMEONE. IT DOESN'T TAKE ALL THAT MUCH; YOU CAN SMILE, SAY "GOOD DAY," HOLD A DOOR OPEN AND DON'T WAIT AROUND FOR A "THANK YOU." YOU DON'T NEED IT. BECAUSE WHEN YOU'RE ALONE YOU'RE GONNA FEEL SO GOOD AND THAT'S ONLY PART OF IT; THAT PERSON WILL GO OUT AND DO SOMETHING NICE FOR SOMEONE ELSE; AND IT'LL SPREAD. AND THIS WHOLE WORLD CAN WIND UP DOING NICE THINGS FOR EACH OTHER AND WE CAN BE THE ONES THAT START IT. LET'S START IT. THAT'S FOR LOVE—IT'S STILL THE BEST AND THIS OLD WORLD CAN USE IT.

This is a little saying I give the audience at the end of each and every show. I believe in it whole-heartedly and feel very strong about each word. I would like this to be my contribution.

ROY CLARK
Country Music Entertainer
Television Personality

LOVE

Without love there is no life.

BILL CONTI
Musical Composer, Arranger

LOVE

All things work together for good for those who love.

PHYLLIS DILLER
Comedian

LOVE

Because nothing less is acceptable.

ANNE HECHE
Actor

LOVE

The first word that came to me was love; and why not? It's the solution to all the world's problems if we could learn to follow that old war protest song of the 1960s:
"COME ON PEOPLE, NOW
LET'S GET TOGETHER
LOVE ONE ANOTHER!"

TONY HILLERMAN
Author

LOVE

I have endeavored to live my life full of love, expressed in my relationships with others and in my career as a singer. Love is at the same time strength and gentleness. I believe that if everyone lived love, there would be no wars, no dissent, only harmony. I've heard it said that love is the only thing you can give away and get back more in return.

FRANKIE LAINE
Singer, Actor

LOVE

It's all there is.

MADELEINE L'ENGLE
Author

LOVE

It's why we're here.

DIANE MEEHAN
Author

LOVE

"KEEP YOUR EYES ON THE STARS AND YOUR FEET ON
THE GROUND. CHARACTER IN THE LONG RUN IS THE
DECISIVE FACTOR IN LIFE."
—Teddy Roosevelt

ANN MILLER
Actress, Dancer

LOVE

No other word I've ever spoken holds so much power when put into action.

Carl Perkins
Rock and Roll Singer
"Blue Suede Shoes"

LOVE

I Corinthians 13
Booker T. Washington said, "I learned the lesson that great men cultivate love, and that only little men cherish a spirit of hatred. I learned that assistance given to the weak makes the one who gives it strong; and that oppression of the unfortunate makes one weak."

John Wooden
Hall of Fame Head Coach, Men's Basketball
Formerly at UCLA

LOVE

I believe one of the most important injunctions in life is to "love" one another. I believe that God intends for us mortal creatures to patch up our differences, to banish selfishness and evil, and to see that none of His creatures are mistreated. That is a tall order and we haven't achieved it, but I think the eternal wisdom proposes that we do so. And I believe these goals are to be attained not only through individual deeds of individual humans but in society as well and in the social structures that we create.

JAMES C. WRIGHT
Former Speaker of the House
United States House of Representatives

LOVE

Without love, life doesn't make sense.

JOLANTA KWASNIEWSKA
President, Communication Without Borders
Wife of the President of Poland
Warsaw, Poland

LOVE

APPROACHING THE WORLD WITH LOVE RATHER THAN WITH FEAR

You generously—and from the perspective of love—gave yourself to us when you participated in the conference "Acts of Service, A Discussion of Religion and Public Life" sponsored by the University of California Santa Barbara and La Casa de Maria Retreat Center, June 1, 2001.

The word (phrase) was attributed to Father Henri Nouwen by a panelist the following day of the conference, Rev. Anne Howard. She described it as a life-defining phrase which she had learned as a divinity student at Harvard. Anne frequently ministers to me. For me, it is grace, a daily gift, which enables us to be in the world with love; thus, acts of service are done in love.

CONGRESSWOMAN LOIS CAPPS
Member of the United States House of Representatives
Represents California District 21

LOVE

It makes the world go round and without it everything is hollow.

VAIRA VIKE-FREIBERGA
President of Latvia

LOVE

I love to read
I try to love my neighbor as myself
I love my family
And most of all I love our God.

BARBARA BUSH
Former First Lady of the United States

LOVE

Love has a lot of power in it. In the years of my performing and recording, love is prevalent; it touches the heart!

ISAAC HAYES
Musician, Singer, Songwriter

LOVE

Without it...where *would* we be?

MEREDITH BAXTER
Actor

LOVE

You need to "love" your family to have a happy life.
You need to "love" your job to contribute positively every day.
You need to "love" everyone around you so you can have a positive
relationship with all
Love conquers everything!

INDRA NOOYI
President and Chief Executive Officer
Pepsico, Inc.

LOVE

LOVE ONE ANOTHER

Those are the words used by Christ at the Last Supper when he told the Apostles, "love one another as I have loved you."
On a trip to lecture in India last year I discovered that these words were on the tomb of Mother Teresa in Calcutta. Her appropriation of these words was indeed a very striking manifestation of her love for humanity.

FATHER ROBERT F. DRINAN, S.J.
Professor of Law, Georgetown University Law Center
Former Member of the United States House of Representatives

LOVE AND RESPECT

GIVE LOVE AND RESPECT TO ALL IN THE WORLD.

This is how I feel.

JOHN AGAR
Actor

LOYALTY

JAMES CARVILLE
Political Consultant, Television Commentator, Author

LOYALTY

Loyalty reflects commitment.
Commitment reflects character.
Thus, the object and depth of one's loyalty reflect one's character.

SENATOR TOM HARKIN
United States Senator from Iowa

LOYALTY

I particularly dislike the use of the word "hate."

SENATOR RUSSELL B. LONG
Former United States Senator from Louisiana

LOYALTY

When I was a jockey, half a century ago, I like to think I was loyal to those for whom I rode; while I was equally pleased when those people were loyal to me. I'm glad to say most of them were too.

DICK FRANCIS
Author

LOYALTY

"Loyalty" is my favorite word; it needs no explanation.
My favorite phrase is "Walk in the other man's shoes." I have always tried to feel, think, and wonder what makes the other person tick. What's it like in *their* shoes?

LARRY KING
Television Personality, Author
Host of *Larry King Live* on CNN-TV

LOYALTY

Commitment.

Teach your child responsibility and they'll teach themselves everything else. This is not original by me; I picked this up somewhere.

It is better to suffer for doing good than for doing evil (1 Peter 3:11).

Most needed scripture verse: "Good name is better to be chosen than great riches!" (From elementary school and Proverbs 22:1)

S. TRUETT CATHY
Founder and Chair of Chik-Fil-A

LOYALTY

I have never lost an enemy or forgotten a friend.

CINDY ADAMS
Gossip Columnist

MANAGERS

THERE IS NO SUCH THING AS A MATURE MARKET,
THERE ARE ONLY BAD MANAGERS.

Regardless of the environment, the growth of a company is directly
proportionate to the commitment to development, ambition,
courage, and competence of those who manage.

PIERRE BELLON
Chairman and Chief Executive Officer, Sodexho Alliance
Montigny-le-Bretonneux, France

MARRIAGE

YOU ONLY GET OUT OF A MARRIAGE WHAT YOU PUT
INTO IT, BUT IT COMES BACK GIFT WRAPPED.

DR. JOYCE D. BROTHERS
Psychologist
Television personality

MELLIFLUOUS

Mellifluous is one of the most beautiful words in all of English. Roll it around on your tongue—from the Latin words for "honey" and "to flow," it's a delicious word that truly lives up to its meaning, a word literally "flowing with honey."

MARTHA BARNETTE
Writer, Journalist

MEMORY

YOU CANNOT REAP WHAT YOU DO NOT SOW.

I value both.

SENATOR BOB KERREY
President of New School University, Former Governor of Nebraska and Former United States Senator from Nebraska Bronze Star Recipient for Service in Vietnam

MEZZO FORTE

I always felt whether in my own profession or in the more difficult profession of life, it is always good to charge in, in a positive manner but also have a braking system to prevent train wrecks.

SKITCH HENDERSON
Musical Composer, Conductor

MIND

THE POWER OF THE MIND IS EVERYTHING.

JACKIE COLLINS
Author

MISCHIEF

I spend much of my life among schoolchildren and it is the natural prerogative of childhood to introduce as many particles of joyful mischief to the world as possible. History grows bored with relatively docile characters such as Tom Sawyer, but it celebrates the misbehavior of Huck Finn. Long live the mischievous!

JONATHAN KOZOL
Author, Educator

MISFORTUNE

NO MISFORTUNE WHICH DOES NOT OFFER A CHANCE FOR LEARNING AND RESETTING PRIORITIES IN LIFE

OTMAR ISSING
Member of the Executive Board and Chief Economist
European Central Bank
Germany

MODERATION

I have found it to be generally a sound rule in all aspects of life.

ALLEN DRURY
Actor

MOLIMINOUS PISMIRE

I like the word *moliminous,* an obsolete term meaning "important," and *pismire,* which could be translated literally as "pissant" but works better as a derisive term for small-minded people. If I referred to, say, an arrogant senator or a haughty rich person as a moliminous pismire, you might translate that as a self-important little twerp. I love the descriptive humor of such words. They're almost like verbal sallies, rapier thrusts. It's a shame such words as these have become antiques; they're too colorful to be wasted.

JOHN EGERTON
Author

MONKEYDANCE

The greatest threat facing the continuation of human life on this planet is overpopulation. It is the root cause all other problems may be attributed to.

Those who would oppose birth control, abortion, and timely sex education for preadolescent children and who would endorse abstinence, celibacy, monogamy, and other high ideals of moral conduct must understand one basic fact. The human is an oversexed creature. Some believe that this is because God told us to go forth and multiply at a time when the population of the world could be numbered in the thousands. Others would claim we are animals and the ability to breed faster than our predators could slay us permitted us to survive and thrive. However unpleasant, facts must be faced, not fought.

For a very fortunate few who are in love with someone who is in love with them, human intimacy is truly romantic lovemaking. For the rest of us, who are merely rubbing our sex itch, what we are doing is nothing more than a monkeydance. A dance which very few of us are willing to sit out.

RANDALL HUGH CRAWFORD
Cartoonist

MORE

MORE TO COME...

Although this phrase is often cheapened by appearing at the intermission of a TV program, etc. still it suggests to me a powerful insight—the openness of history, the ongoingness of God's tussle with humanity, the ever deeper meaning of live in human life.

Dr. Harvey Cox Jr.
Hollis Professor of Divinity, Harvard Divinity School
Author

MOTHER

There is a reverence about it and a universality. One's own mother, and Mother Earth—one who we would profane at the cost of our own humanity; the other which we profane at the cost of all humanity.

Walter Cronkite
Journalist, Former Anchor for the CBS-TV Evening News
"The most respected man in America"

MUCH

MUCH HAS BEEN GIVEN TO YOU, AND MUCH IS EXPECTED OF YOU.

One of my favorite phrases...that I heard from my parents many times. I'm not sure of its origin. It may well be biblical, but it was my parents' way of saying to me and my brother that we had been blessed with good parents, strong values, and a proud ethnic heritage, and we had a responsibility to make a real contribution to the community and state and country that had welcomed our parents to this country.

These days I try to convey that same sense of responsibility to the students I teach at Northwestern and during the winter at UCLA. We're producing some fine young people these days, and I want to see more and more of them pursue public service as a career where we can "expect much of them," too.

MICHAEL S. DUKAKIS
University Professor, Former Governor of Massachusetts
1988 Democratic Nominee for the President of the United States

MUSIC

MUSIC IS LOVE IN SEARCH OF A WORD.

Since love is such an esoteric expression, and for centuries most have failed in their attempts adequately to describe it, I have discovered in my life that I could express my love for those I care for as well as strangers through the power of music. Music has given my love its "word."

VICTORIA LIVENGOOD
Opera Singer

MUTUAL RESPECT

I give you those words because they are a crucial principle in the relations between men and women. They will also lead to a better society and a stronger democracy.

THE HONORABLE PATRICK DEWAEI
Minister-President
Government of Flanders
Belgium

NETWORK

It is such a powerful element in personal happiness and success. My wife, Gayle Hallgren-Rezac, Judy Thomson, and I have just written a book on the subject based on my twenty years studying, observing, and practicing the art of "positive" networking. *The Frog and Prince: Secrets of Positive Networking* is all about discovering what you can do for someone else. It is not only a "how-to" book, it delves into the "why" as well. I believe it is the first book to marry the art of networking with the amazing new science of networks (which builds upon the fairly recent mathematical proof the CE small worlds phenomenon).

From page 168: "It is a voyage of discovery that never ends. Always be aware of the network and its reach: it is always on. Understand that positive networking flows from the secrets and the steps of the network dance. Therefore, practice, practice, practice. Finally, participate and be a contributor. In time, you—and those you touch—will experience the magic of the random and unexpected good things that come from positive networking done well."

DARCY REZAC
Managing Director, The Vancouver Board of Trade
Author

NEVER

YOU NEVER CAN TELL.

Somebody from the financial world asked the former Bishop of
Massachusetts, John Coburn, where he would like to invest his
money. Before answering, the advisor said, "My father always used
to tell me your guess is as good as mine." Then he said, "Bishop,
have you got a piece of wisdom for me?" John's reply was, "You
never can tell." Frankly, Welton, that's about as good advice as I
can give to anybody who lives in a world of total ambiguity such
as we find ourselves in at the moment.

CONGRESSMAN AMO HOUGHTON
Member of the United States House of Representatives
Representative of Congressional District 31 in New York

NEVER

These are the words of Winston Churchill's shortest speech:
"Never give in, never give in, never, never, never!"

ROSS PEROT
Chairman, Perot Systems
Independent Candidate for the President of the United States,
1992

NICE

BE NICE.

It takes very little effort to be nice to people and kindness is
usually returned tenfold.

JEANNE SHAHEEN
Former Governor of New Hampshire

NICE

IT'S NICE TO BE IMPORTANT
BUT IT'S MORE IMPORTANT TO BE NICE!!

People in the world have a tendency to place their importance above humility.

TRINI LOPEZ
Songwriter, Actor, Singer, *If I Had a Hammer*
"Mr. La Bamba"

NIGHTMARE

OUR LONG NATIONAL NIGHTMARE IS OVER.

As I told you in my office, the above sentence from my acceptance speech, after taking the Oath in the East Room of the White House, is the most meaningful to me. The words appropriately ended the Watergate era and ushered in a new and brighter period in America's history.

GERALD R. FORD
Thirty-Eighth President of the United States

NITWIT

It just is the perfect description and sound for those folks in life who drive you nuts.

AL ROKER
Weatherman on NBC-TV's *Today Show*, Author

NONVIOLENCE

To me, the greatest need we all face in these times is to put away our violence, to abolish war and nuclear weapons, to dismantle every injustice, and to create a culture of peace and justice. In other words, we need to become people of nonviolence, to build a culture of nonviolence, and to worship the God of nonviolence. Mahatma Gandhi and Dr. King spent their lives calling us to embrace the wisdom and practice of nonviolence. I believe that if we pursue nonviolence in the depths of our hearts and in every facet of society, we will discover not only the meaning of love, peace and life itself, but the presence of God in our midst.

REV. JOHN DEAR, S.J.
Jesuit Priest, Pastor, Peace Activist, Author
Former Executive Director of The Fellowship of Reconciliation

OHANA

Ohana means family. I grew up in Hawaii with lots of caring and family. We were all very close. People in Hawaii will make everyone feel like family and that we are all connected. Now that I'm grown, with my own family, Ohana has even deeper meaning for me.

KELLY PRESTON
Actor, *View from the Top*

ONE

My first cover story for *The Observer* was entitled "How Big Is One." Everything begins with one—one person can make a difference and everyone should try. The wee small voice of *The Observer* echoes around the country, one small publication speaking truth to power.

FORREST J. (FROSTY) TROY
Publisher and Editor, *The Observer*
A weekly newspaper in Oklahoma

ONE

ONE PERSON CAN MAKE A DIFFERENCE.

My sixth grade teacher, a woman named Marguerite Holcomb, found the wherewithal to provide each student with enough balsa wood to build a glider of three-foot wingspan. She then held a competition to see which gliders could fly farthest, highest, and longest in time. After having Mrs. Holcomb as a teacher, I never swayed for very long from seeking a career in aviation. This is a trivial example of one person making a difference. I am sure that you can find many others in your personal and professional lives.

WILLIAM H. DANA
Astronaut, NASA Test Pilot
Pilot of the final X-15 flight
Recipient of NASA'S Distinguished Service Medal

ONOMATOPOEIA

This (has been) my favorite word ever since I first heard it back in high school. Inez Hughes, my English teacher that year, would say it aloud for us—her head pitched slightly back, her chin jutted forward, her eyes full of playfulness, as she proclaimed: "Nothing gives greater pleasure, boys and girls, than the music of language, and nothing is more rewarding than to discover that **you**, boys and girls, can make such music, yourself. O-no-mat-o-poeia"—the syllables came rolling from her lips like bubbles—"is yours for the making!" Even now, almost fifty years later, I love to say the word aloud; it is like poetry to me.

BILL MOYERS
Television journalist, Host of *NOW* on PBS-TV, Author
Former White House Press Secretary for President Lyndon B. Johnson

OPEN

More minds of more people everywhere need to be open (about many things).

ALLAN E. GOODMAN
President and Chief Executive Officer
Institute of International Education

OPPORTUNITY

Opportunity is what America is about. Opportunity is what millions of immigrants came here to find—the chance to build a better life, if not for them, then for their children and grandchildren.

Opportunity means the right to succeed *and* the right to fail—and the right to try again when you fall short. Societies based on opportunity, where individual achievement is honored and hard work is rewarded, are the most productive, prosperous, and humane societies on earth. Without opportunity, people lose hope. And so "opportunity" is my word because it feeds the body and the soul, and it is the greatest gift one generation can ever leave to another.

THOMAS J. DONOHUE
President and Chief Executive Officer
United States Chamber of Commerce

OYEE

NO MORE SHACKS.

Oyee! This is a yell of affirmation from Zaire in Central Africa. When a speaker stands up to speak in a public gathering in Zaire, he typically yells out, "Oyee!!" The audience then responds in unison, "Oyee!!"

In Habitat for Humanity we have incorporated that yell of exuberance and affirmation and I, especially, use it a lot at Habitat house dedication services. Invariably, yelling this word back and forth between the speaker and the audience creates great excitement and joy among everybody present. It gives us all encouragement to continue in the good work that God has given us of eliminating poverty housing and homelessness from the face of the earth.

This phrase is the name of one of the books I have written about the ministry of Habitat for Humanity. It states in succinct form the goal of the ministry of Habitat for Humanity; namely, to get rid of all shacks and other substandard housing, and replace that substandard housing with modest but good and solid homes for God's people in need.

The phrase is a rallying cry in this work of Habitat for Humanity, and it energizes all of us to redouble our efforts to accomplish our God-ordained task of ridding the earth of substandard housing and homelessness.

MILLARD FULLER
Founder and President
Habitat for Humanity International

PACE

This is an important part of my philosophy not only in my profession—TV comedy—but also in my outlook on life.

Pace doesn't just mean speed—it means don't waste time on minor issues, but take your time with the important ones. Rest...where you slow down in comedy or life it has greater impact.

JAY SANDRICH
Television Director
The Mary Tyler Moore Show

PACE

PACE YOURSELF.

Life's journey is long and arduous. Change does not occur overnight. We often said during the civil rights movement that ours was not a struggle of a day, a week or a season, it is the struggle of a lifetime. I often say the say the same thing to people today. Don't expect change to occur immediately, it is something you must work toward every day, so pace yourself.

CONGRESSMAN JOHN LEWIS
Member of the United States House of Representatives
Represents the 5th Congressional District of Georgia
Civil Rights Leader and Author

PARTNERSHIP

I believe that it takes all of us—government, business, charitable organizations, and individuals, to do the most important things for our community. Forming successful partnerships has been one of my proudest accomplishments as Mayor of Boston. It has helped us to reduce crime among youth, improve education for our children, and revitalize our neighborhoods.

THOMAS M. MENINO
Mayor of Boston, Massachusetts

PASS

THIS TOO SHALL PASS.

All things move on, good and bad.
Never get too high or too low.

RICK MAJERUS
Head Coach, Men's Basketball
University of Utah

PASS

THIS TOO SHALL PASS.

In my younger days, when things seemed at 6's and 7's, my wonderful mother-in-law would leave a sign on my mirror: "This too shall pass..." That hopeful thought helped me over many bumps in the road.

JUSTICE RUTH BADER GINSBURG
United States Supreme Court Justice

PASSION

UNBELIEVABLE PASSION

It is the inexhaustible fuel that launches and maintains a commitment. And allows it to be manifest in the world.

ROBERT DESIDERIO
Actor, Screenwriter

PATIENCE

Its root means suffering: but to be patient implies to be resourceful. It means starting again after setbacks, and then starting again. It means waiting until an idea is right, or a project properly finished. It is the quality we all need as we reach the end of our lives.

A. S. BYATT
British Author
1990 Booker Prize for *Possession*

PATIENCE

I am one of the most impatient people I know! I have to constantly remind myself that patience is necessary in this lifetime. Without it—I go mad!

MELISSA DYE
Broadway Actor

PATIENCE

PATIENCE, TIMING, POSITIONING

Luck is very important in one's life. But often lucky ones are those who enhance their probabilities of being lucky by patience, timing, and positioning.

VURAL AKISIK
Chairman, Disbank
Turkey

PATRIOTISM

Patriotism has always been an expression of the willingness of an individual to dedicate a certain portion of himself, his talents and energies, to something beyond himself. To adopt for himself, the basic values that have made our nation what it is, and to be willing to struggle—and if necessary to fight—for those values.

GENERAL ALEXANDER HAIG
Secretary of State for the United States in the
Reagan Administration

PEACE

"PEACE, A WORD FROM THE MERCIFUL LORD"
—The Holy Qur'an, Surat Yasin, 36:58

In Heaven, Peace is both a Divine Attribute, and the condition of the people of Heaven, in the Holy Qur'an. One earth, peace of heart, true peace of heart, is what all peoples were born to seek, for there is no happiness without it. It is also, politically, what all nations must strive to accomplish between themselves. The world must thus constantly redouble its efforts to achieve peace in the Middle East.

HIS MAJESTY KING ABDULLAH II BIN AL-HUSSEIN
King of the Royal Hashemite Kingdom of Jordan

PEACE

Hemingway wanted everyone to be brothers and sisters.
We were born for it; and to do good.
I want to be in peace. If I'm not quiet, I don't have peace.*
This is why it was Hemingway's favorite word also.

GREGORIO FUENTES BETANCOURT
Best Friend of Ernest Hemingway
Captain of the *Pilar*, Hemingway's fishing yacht

*Fuentes used the word "quiet" to mean "being where you are and
not being bothered."

PEACE

Give peace a chance.

MARK FREEDMAN
Chef, Mark's on Westover
Greensboro, North Carolina

PEACE, HOPE, AND HEARTSONGS

These are the things we need to remember for ourselves and our world.

MATTIE J. T. STEPANEK
Eleven-year-old poet
Author of *Heartsongs*

PEARL

THE PEARL OF GREAT PRICE

The human heart is in quest of something supremely good that merits our unconditional love, reverence, and service. I believe that God offers this gift to us in his son. See Matthew 13:45-46.

HIS EMINENCE AVERY CARDINAL DULLES, S.J.
Laurence J. McGinley Professor of Religion and Society
Fordham University

205

PERSEVERANCE

I would not be where I am today without perseverance. It took six general elections before I won a seat in the House of Assembly, and as a Leader of my Party—I have faced three elections to hold this post.

THE HONORABLE JENNIFER M. SMITH
Prime Minister of Bermuda

PERSEVERANCE

FRANK OLSON
Chairman, The Hertz Corporation

PERSEVERE

So often in life when things are not going well or great challenges are appearing, if one can just persevere, it is often possible to snatch victory from the jaws of defeat.

NORMAN R. AUGUSTINE
Chairman of the Board, Lockheed Martin Corporation

PERSEVERE

Professor, Yale University
Nobel Laureate in Chemistry

PERSIST

The definition of *persist* is: to go on resolutely in spite of opposition, importunity, or warning. This word describes me and my career. Being a woman in an elected government position you have to be willing to persist if you hope to be successful.

SENATOR MARY L. LANDRIEU
United States Senator from Louisiana

207

PERSIST

I have seen too many gifted people fail to realize their potential because they could not stand rejection or the spectre of failure. I believe there are only two ways to avoid being a "failure."

1. Don't start.
2. Don't quit.

ART LINKLETTER
Television Host, Author

PERSISTENCE

T. BERRY BRAZELTON, M.D.
Pediatrician, Child Development Author
Clinical Professor of Pediatrics Emeritus, Harvard University

PERSISTENCE

Serious setbacks have to be overcome and turned into successes.

ANTHONY GIDDENS, PH.D.
Director, London School of Economics and Political Science
United Kingdom

PERSISTENCE

It is truly the key to success in any area of endeavor.

JOSEPH L. RICE III
Chairman of Clayton, Dubilier & Rice Inc.

PERSPECTIVE

The word implies wide vision and, by extension, fairness and proportion, qualities I admire as necessary to a civilized life. By reminding myself to "keep things in perspective," I can sometimes manage to slow myself down long enough to understand that everything that's going on in my vicinity isn't necessarily either about me or my fault.

MARY-LOU WEISMAN
Author

PICTURE

Because of my dyslexia, I'm enclosing a drawing instead of a word...because "A picture is worth a thousand words!"

MIKE PETERS
Creator of the comic strip "Mother Goose & Grimm"
Cartoonist, *Dayton Daily News*

PLAY

Because I believe God is playful.

FATHER ANDREW GREELEY
Priest, Author
Professor of Social Science, The University of Chicago

PLAYERS

PLAYERS WIN, COACHES DON'T. OUR JOB AS COACHES
IS TO PLACE THE PLAYERS IN THE RIGHT POSITION
TO ENABLE THEM TO WIN.

JACKIE SHERRILL
Head Football Coach
Mississippi State University

POSITIVE

Positive people have hope. With hope and faith you can
overcome any hardship or disappointment. Keep the faith
by becoming a positive.

TIMOTHY C. MCDONOUGH
Mayor of Hope, New Jersey

POSITIVE

BE POSITIVE.

We can all be much more productive if we maintain a positive outlook and attitude as we go through life. This type of positive leadership is good for everyone.

GERALD D. JENNINGS
Mayor of Albany, New York

POSSIBLE

With hard work and diligence, nearly all things are "possible."

ROBERT S. MILLER
Chairman and Chief Executive Officer
Bethlehem Steel Corporation

POSSIBILITIES

I'm an optimist. There are always possibilities.

BETTY DeGENERES
Motivational Speaker, Mother of Ellen DeGeneres

PRAISE

Alex Hailey, author of *Roots*, lived his life by six words: Find the Good and Praise it. In all of the time that I knew him, he never had a bad word to say about someone's race or background. And he wouldn't put up with those who were busy finding everything wrong with America. This was always a powerful message, coming from the grandson of slaves, the man whose brother went to a segregated law school, the man who wrote *The Autobiography of Malcolm X* as well as the story of *Roots*. Find the good and praise it.

I thought about those words on a February afternoon in Henning, Tennessee in 1992 when an African flute played a beautiful melody and we buried Alex Hailey. We stood next to the front porch where his grandma and great aunts had told stories of their ancestors that Alex later turned into the best-watched miniseries ever on television. On his grave marker, in front of that house are those six words. Find the good and praise it.

SENATOR LAMAR ALEXANDER
United States Senator from Tennessee
Former Governor of Tennessee

PREPARATION

In my opinion, a successful career in the performing arts is dependent upon three factors: God given talent, luck, and preparation. Of the three, preparation is the one which the aspiring artist can control completely.

ROBERTA PETERS
Singer

PREPARED

BE PREPARED AND THINK POSITIVELY.

I learned early in my career during difficult rehearsals at the opera that this motto was very helpful.

ROBERT MERRILL
Opera Singer

PRESENT

"THE PAST IS HISTORY, THE FUTURE IS MYSTERY, AND
THAT IS WHY THIS MOMENT IS CALLED 'THE PRESENT.'"
—Dr. Deepak Chopra
Seven Spiritual Laws of Success

In life we tend to look at our past as a foreteller of our future.
I know I have been guilty of thinking a past failure meant only
failure in the future—But we should only focus on *today* and
being our absolute best. If we can do that with a grateful attitude,
we cannot fail. My mother used to tell me to "Bloom where you
are planted," which really is the same as Dr. Chopra's quote when
you think about it. Good advice I've tried to take.

HOLLY DUNN
Country Music Artist

PRESENT
YESTERDAY IS HISTORY; THE FUTURE IS A MYSTERY;
TODAY IS A GIFT, THAT'S WHY IT'S CALLED THE PRESENT.

ANN DOUGLAS
Philanthropist, Wife of Kirk Douglas

PRESSURE

PRESSURE TURNS COAL INTO DIAMONDS!

GARY BARNETT
Head Football Coach
The University of Colorado

PRINCIPLES

We must adjust to changing times, but cling to unchanging principles.

JIMMY CARTER
Thirty-Ninth President of the United States
Nobel Peace Laureate, 2002

PROFESSIONAL

It is my most treasured expression for an actor or crew member who knows his/her craft, who has training and experience, who performs whole-heartedly and without nonsense, who is dedicated to the work or the project, with whom it is a joy to work and to be associated, who is in all ways, the best of the best, and who, last but far from least, is simply fun and rewarding to be around. I feel totally blessed when I encounter one. My use of the word *professional* is the highest praise I can give.

DELBERT MANN
Academy Award-Winning Movie Director
Marty and *All's Quiet on the Western Front*

PROMISE

Promise is a word that embodies the attributes of our nation. Promise is the Opportunity granted to each of us to achieve the American Dream. Promise is the potential that each of us has to succeed, regardless of our origins. Promise is the covenant between our citizens and our government to ensure that each of us has equal access to the pursuit of happiness. And most of all, promise is the spirit with which we undertake all of our challenges, both personal and collective.

SENATOR JON S. CORZINE
United States Senator from New Jersey

PUBLIC

PUBLIC SERVANT

There is no higher secular calling than public service—not politics or political office, but service to the nation, the society, the community. It is the foundational principle of a democratic republic.

SENATOR GARY HART
Former United States Senator from Colorado

PURSUIT

PURSUIT OF TRUTH

I believe the modern concept of "possessing" the truth has created more conflict in the history of humankind than any other. It leads to a "closed" mind. Pursuit is open, honest, and enhancing.

DR. ARUN GANDHI
Founder Director of the M.K. Gandhi Institute for Nonviolence
Author
Grandson of Mahatma Gandhi

QUALITY

The only word I remember from any commencement speech I listened to. The speaker at my Ph.D. commencement (May '78, I don't remember his name) made the point that we all would leave with the same piece of paper—but not the same degree. The single thing that distinguished our piece of paper from someone else's was the *quality* with which we had imbued it—through the quality of our work and motivations. Though the certificate might look the same to an uncritical eye, he assured us that the world would quickly discern the differences in quality behind each.

DR. KATHRYN SULLIVAN
Astronaut, Mission Specialist on two Shuttle Flights
Payload Commander on the first Spacelab Mission dedicated to
NASA's Mission to Planet Earth
President and Chief Executive Officer
Center of Science and Industry

REACH

REACH FOR THE STARS.

BARONESS SUSAN GREENFIELD
Director, The Royal Institute of Great Britain
United Kingdom

REACH

A MAN'S REACH SHOULD EXCEED HIS GRASP,
OR WHAT'S A HEAVEN FOR?

I imagine the quote I have used the most with my team and
family is "A man's reach should exceed his grasp, or what's a
Heaven for?" I hope this helps.

JOSEPH V. PATERNO
Head Football Coach
The Pennsylvania State University

REACT

IT'S NOT WHAT HAPPENS...IT'S HOW YOU REACT.

DON CRIQUI
Television Sportscaster

RECKON

I offer this word to you because:
It leaves room for questioning. In Mississippi, where I grew up, if one said, "I reckon so" about some subject it meant that the speaker was sure of something and at the same time he was not absolutely positive. To me it's a theological word. It's kind of like faith. As opposed to belief. Belief is passive. It doesn't require us to do anything. "I believe a whale swallowed a man." So what? Faith is active. By belief I do nothing but recite what I believe. By faith I go into the world and try to turn it right side up. The theology of reckoning. I'm suspicious of the theology of certitude. If I reckon, I can tolerate anything and discuss anything. In certitude, well, "God said it, I believe it, that settles it." So says the bumper sticker.

WILL D. CAMPBELL
Preacher, Writer

222

REJECT/ACCEPT

REJECT, EMPHATICALLY, THAT FOR WHICH THERE IS
NO EVIDENCE. ACCEPT, TENTATIVELY ONLY THAT
FOR WHICH THERE IS AT LEAST SOME EVIDENCE.

There are those, perhaps most, who uncritically believe as true,
propositions for which there is no evidence. They infuriate me
because they reject their most precious gift, the ability to think.

HERBERT A. HAUPTMAN
Nobel Laureate in Chemistry, 1985
Hauptman Woodward Medical Research Institution Inc.

RELATIONSHIPS

Once I was asked, "What is important to be happy?" I was surrounded by my family members at that moment, and I was happy. So I answered spontaneously, relationships—good relationships with your family. I have reflected on this answer quite often since then and have kept it at the forefront of my conscience. Now I try to enjoy a good relationship with my surroundings and within myself.

AYE AYE THANT
Daughter of former United Nations Secretary General U Thant

RESILIENCE

I found it a challenge to choose just one word. Determination, hope, compassion, resilience, calm, wisdom, humor and inspiration all came to mind. In the end, I chose **resilience**.

The resilience of the human spirit; the resilience of individuals, groups and nations of peoples, who, despite all odds, go forward in life with determination, hope, compassion, calm, wisdom, humor and inspiration, while holding fast the very center of their being. This collective resilience never ceases to inspire me.

MAUREEN MCGOVERN
Musician, Singer
Oscar-Winning Song, "The Morning After"

RESILIENT

In every endeavor and all of our tasks and challenges, you must be resilient to see them through. In all things, you must be patient, strong, and resilient to be successful.

CAMERON H. BONIFAY
Former General Manager of the Pittsburgh Pirates
Major League Baseball Team

RESIST

CLAY BENNETT
Editorial Cartoonist
The Christian Science Monitor

RESPECT

Everything begins with Respect.

KEITH JACKSON
Television Sportscaster, ABC-TV

RESPECT

More than love, admiration, or anything. Whether it be for others or God—you can tell when someone has respect.

WAYLON JENNINGS
Country Music Singer

RESPECT

Everyone deserves to be treated with respect, no matter what is his/her station in life or the circumstances under which an interaction occurs. I continually put myself in the position of others and ask how I would like to be treated—"with respect" usually surfaces, then, more explicitly, according to "The Golden Rule."

KAREN A. HOLBROOK
President of Ohio State University

RESPECT

True respect—for another, an idea, the earth, ourselves—seems to me to hold large measures of appreciation and awe, with a touch of joy. It has nothing to do with fear. Lack of respect seems to fill the world today, replaced by a joyless arrogance that demands war. I see no way to change this but I wish it would change.

S. J. ROZAN
Author

RESPECT

Respect is part of the equation of wisdom. Intelligence in itself, is not sufficient. Many words describe the ability of doing things cleverly: good judgment, perception, astuteness, knowledge, understanding, common sense, insight, and many others. But none really include the notion of respect.

I understand the word "Respect" as a positive and proactive attitude towards our fellow human and, in general, towards our Environment. Sustainable environment policy is nothing new, in fact, but an attitude of Respect. Respect for the others, Respect for their well-being, their religion and their culture, Respect for their differences, Respect for their environment, Respect for our world. Respect is a heartily feelings approach, not an intellectual posture. Respect is an attitude when listening and accepting, understanding, sharing and embracing, or even challenging viewpoints that might be certainties for many others.

Respect should be a priority principal in many decisions taken in good faith.

HRH PRINCE JEAN OF LUXEMBOURG
Chairman, Ozonia
Senior Vice President, Ondeo Nalco
France

RESPECT

Until we learn to *respect* all other peoples, there will continue to be hostilities, wars, and destruction.

On the other hand:

My wife Hildred of many years (61), a bright lady and a wonderful sculptor, disagrees with my choice of "word." She believes the most important word is "**hope.**" If you deprive people of "**hope,**" they have nothing to look forward to and the future is meaningless. (And I have the utmost **respect** for my wife.)

SHERWOOD SCHWARTZ
Emmy Award-Winning Writer
Creator of *Gilligan's Island* and *The Brady Bunch*

RESPONSIBILITY

Responsibility is the basis of defining contribution. As knowledgeable workers, each of us needs to understand where we fit and what is our contribution. It is the basis of self-respect as well as the respect of others.

JOHN W. BACHMANN
Managing Partner, Edward Jones

RESULTS

TANGIBLE RESULTS

The fundamental value our Management Consulting firm,
A.T. Kearney stands for: A consultant, life-long source of energy
and commitment for my colleagues and me.

DIETMAR OSTERMANN
Chief Executive Officer, A.T. Kearney

REVERENCE

REVERENCE AND RESPONSIBILITY

They name qualities essential for a holy/wholesome life.

NANCY MAIRS
Author

RIPPLES

This is from a quote by Robert Kennedy. He talked about that wherever someone does an act of kindness or fights injustice that it sends ripples out into the world. And it is those ripples intersecting and interacting with each other and reaching critical mass that will change the world.

BEN COHEN
Co-founder of Ben & Jerry's Ice Cream
Founder of Business Leaders for Sensible Priorities

RISK

TO TAKE A RISK.

I believe that to take a risk has a special meaning in my life! To stand up and be counted is important.

DR. RUTH K. WESTHEIMER
Psychosexual Therapist, Pioneer in Media Psychology
Author

ROADS

"TWO ROADS DIVERGED IN A WOOD AND I—
I TOOK THE ONE LESS TRAVELLED BY,
AND THAT HAS MADE ALL THE DIFFERENCE."
—Robert Frost

Think differently, act differently, be different, and make a difference. To do this you need to take the road less traveled by, and this is what my company Ferd and I try to do.

JOHAN H. ANDRESEN JR.
Owner and Chief Executive Officer
Ferd
Norway

SEE

TO SEE (verb)

- Seer
- Visionary
- Clairvoyant
- "The inner eye...is the Bliss of Solitude" (Wordsworth)
- "For now we see through a glass, darkly..." (New Testament)

MARGARET ATWOOD
Author

SEE

TO SEE, LOOK OFF-CENTER; TO HEAR, COVER
YOUR EARS; STRETCH IN THE MORNING; KILL THE
CONCEPT OF YEARS; EAT WHATEVER YOU WANT;
FEED THE HUNGRY.

You asked.

CLYDE EDGERTON
Author

SELF

THE ELEVENTH COMMANDMENT: "THOU SHALT
NOT TAKE THYSELF TOO SERIOUSLY."

I like self-effacing people. Humility looks good on people,
especially great achievers. I've always had a problem with egos.

RALPH EMERY
Country Music Personality
Talk Show Host

SELF-CRITICISM

I find that the ability to continuously and systematically analyze oneself and recognize one's internal faults and failures is the best way to ensure personal, professional, and ethical growth. People that give themselves to this task and embrace the difficulties associated with it tend to be successful in many facets of their lives, including maintaining a sense of humility, humanity, and perspective; peoples and nations that are able to look at their errors hopefully become better neighbors and improve the human condition.

DANIEL LUBETZKY
Founder of PeaceWorks Foundation
Founder and President of PeaceWorks LLC
"Food as a recipe for peace in the Middle East"

SELF-DENIAL

I love the story of a woman holding a young son in her arms who inquired of General Robert E. Lee what she could do to make sure that her son became a great man. Lee replied, "Teach him to deny himself."

We are living in a time where there is not a great deal of self-denial unless it is forced self-denial caused by poverty or prison. It is one of the old values that seems to be slipping out of use.

GRIFFIN B. BELL
Lawyer, Former Attorney General of the United States

SELF-KNOWLEDGE

SENATOR BILL BRADLEY
Former United States Senator from New Jersey
All Star and Hall of Fame National Basketball Association Player
New York Knicks

SELF-WORTH

NEVER CONFUSE YOUR SELF-WORTH WITH YOUR
PROFESSIONAL SUCCESS OR FAILURE.

Mama repeated this over and over during Susan's and my child-
hoods. It is an impossibly difficult thing to follow in the grip of a
crisis but good to have softly repeating in the back of the brain.

CHERRY JONES
Actor, Winner of the Tony Award for her lead role in *The Heiress*

SERENDIPITY

This is very important in science where the unexpected often leads
to the breakthrough discovered.

RICHARD J. ROBERTS
1993 Nobel Laureate in Medicine (discovery of split genes)
Vice President for Research, New England Biolabs, Inc.

SERENDIPITY

My life has so often been enriched by the unexpected.

SHELDON GLASHOW
Nobel Laureate in Physics, 1979
Distinguished Visiting Scientist, Boston University

SERVE

The Lord was asked how one achieves eternal life. He gave a
very simple explanation: "I was thirsty and you gave me to drink;
I was hungry and gave me to eat; I was imprisoned and you visited
me; I was naked and you clothed me; I was homeless and you
took me in." He then said: "Is that eternal life?" He responded:
"What so ever you did for one of these my least brethren, you did
it for Me." Heaven is achieved by serving others.

FATHER THEODORE M. HESBURGH, C.S.C.
President Emeritus, University of Notre Dame

SERVE

I do.

ADMIRAL ELMO RUSSELL ZUMWALT JR.
United States Navy
Chief of Naval Operations and Member of Joint Chiefs of Staff,
1970–1974

SERVICE

LIFETIME HABITS OF SERVICE

One of the major goals of higher of education is to foster this goal.

REVEREND DR. EDWARD A. MALLOY
President, University of Notre Dame

SEX

I suppose none of us would be here without it. But it goes further
than that. Goose and gander do not share the same desires—
A woman wants one man to fulfill all her needs.
A man wants all women to fulfill only one need.

GENE SIMMONS
Rock Singer, "The Demon of the Rock Band *KISS*"

SHALOM

It not only means Peace and is a way of greeting, it has
connotations of wholeness, of everything being in its place
and nothing lacking.

RABBI HAROLD KUSHNER
Author
Rabbi Laureate of Temple Israel
Natick, Massachusetts

SING

Because it gives life.

THEODORE BIKEL
Emmy Award Winning Actor, Folk Musician, Author

SMILE

A smile is the reflection of enjoyment. Life, being precious and short, should be enjoyed. We should always be ready for a smile and, more important, ready to induce a smile on those with whom we associate.

TIM O'BRIEN
Television Correspondent and Journalist

SMILE

...YOU MAKE ME SMILE WITH MY HEART.

In *My Funny Valentine*, Lorenz Hart, one of America's great lyricists, simplified life's most complex emotion. Offering neither "big" words, nor "heavy" psychological insight, he defined the lover's emotion with those seven words!

JULIUS LA ROSA
Actor, Singer

SOCIAL

SOCIAL RESPONSIBILITY

It is a notion that academics, governments, nongovernment organizations, and the private sector must unite behind in order to fulfill our obligations to improve conditions for most of the world's population.

DAVID J. STERN
Commissioner, National Basketball Association

SOLIDARITY

YOLANDA KAKABADSE NAVARRO
President, The World Conservation Union
Switzerland

SOLITUDE

Ralph Emerson wrote in his essay entitled *Self-Reliance* that "it is easy in the world to live after the world's opinion; it is easy solitude to live after our own; but the great man is he who in the midst of the crowd keeps with perfect sweetness and independence of solitude." I have seen men in positions of power and millionaires without it; I have seen prisoners and homeless people with it, and have never had any doubt who's the richer.

JAYSON BLAIR
Journalist

244

SOMEBODY

EVERYBODY IS SOMEBODY, AND EVERYBODY
NEEDS AN OPPORTUNITY TO BE SOMEBODY.

As we strive as coaches to maximize the potential of an athlete,
it is vital to remember that everybody is important and should
be treated with dignity and respect, and should be given the
opportunity and encouragement to be somebody, or in other
words, to be the best that person can be.

VINCENT (VINCE) J. DOOLEY
Athletic Director, Former Football Coach of the University of Georgia

SOULS

IT'S NOT ENOUGH TO WIRE THE WORLD IF WE
SHORT-CIRCUIT OUR SOULS.

In this brave new world of cyber technology we must never
forget the human equation.

TOM BROKAW
Anchor of *NBC Nightly News*, Author

STAY

STAY IN THERE AND PITCH!

FRANK BORMAN
Astronaut, Commander on *Apollo 8*
Chairman, Chief Executive Officer, and President of the
Patlex Corporation

STICK-TO-ITIVENESS

I like this word. My mother taught me this word. I apply it daily
although it is not always easy. Definition: noun. Propensity to follow
through in a determined manner. Dogged persistence born of obligation and stubbornness. Stick-to-itiveness is as important as anything
else but it does not just happen. You have to develop the habit of
persevering even when you don't want to and it would be easier to just
give up. Any fight worth fighting will require stick-to-itiveness.

ERIN BROCKOVICH
Activist
Subject of the movie *Erin Brockovich* in which
her role was played by Julia Roberts

STOP

ON YOUR MARKS, GET SET...STOP!

By turning a famous sports phrase on its head, it best
captures the message and the hope of the Olympic Truce initiative.
It highlights the potential of sport to bring together peoples
of different ethnic and cultural backgrounds in peaceful
competition and to promote peace and understanding during
what is arguably the biggest nonpolitical gathering of Humanity,
the Olympic Games.

STAVROS LAMBRINIDIS
Director, International Olympic Truce Centre
Greece

STRENGTH/ GENTLENESS

THE STRENGTH OF GENTLENESS

This was a quality attributed to me by the actress
Shirley MacLaine in 1972.
I have always treasured it.

SENATOR GEORGE MCGOVERN
Former United States Senator from South Dakota
Democratic Nominee for President of the United States in 1972

STRUGGLE

The forces of evil are so pervasive—greed, ignorance, lust, anger, self-absorption, self-righteousness, sloth, weakness—and so self-degenerating that constant struggle is required to give decency a chance.

ROGER WILKINS
Clarence J. Robinson Professor of History and American Culture
George Mason University
Former Chair of the Pulitzer Prize Board
Civil Rights Activist

SUCCESS

SUCCESS IS A JOURNEY, NOT A DESTINATION.

LAVELL EDWARDS
Former Head Football Coach
Brigham Young University

SUCCESS/FAILURE

SUCCESS ISN'T FINAL.
FAILURE ISN'T FATAL.

DON SHULA
Hall of Fame Head Football Coach
Baltimore Colts and Miami Dolphins

SUFFICIENCY

I HAVE A GRACIOUS SUFFICIENCY.

My great-grandmother taught me to say this when declining
another helping of food. However, I believe it applies to many
occasions. Most of us have had a "gracious sufficiency."

JOANNE WOODWARD
Actor

250

SUN

THE SUN DOESN'T SHINE ON THE SAME DOG'S TAIL
ALL THE TIME.

It says to me to not despair at the bad times, and to enjoy the
good because change is a coming!

JEFF FOXWORTHY
Comedian, Television Personality

SUPERCALIFRAGILIS-
TICEXPIALIDOCIOUS

My brother Robert and I wrote the music lyrics to the film
Mary Poppins and this long word was the title to one of our songs.
When we won two Academy Awards for our score (in 1965), in
our acceptance we said, "...when there's nothing left to say, all you
can say is supercalifragilisticexpialidocious!!!"

RICHARD M. SHERMAN
Musician, Academy Award-Winning Songwriter

SURPRISED

ENJOY BEING SURPRISED. BE PREPARED.

I am 65, an engineer, the head of a big group, and I don't need more than these two sentences as inspiration.

BELMIRO DE AZEVEDO
President and Chief Executive Officer, Sonae SGPS SA, Portugal

SURREAL

The word is surreal. We know the "world" and "truth." There are only perceptions. These are fantasies in the cerebral complex. Pain is not "real." Sleep is not "real." Logic in most cases is not "real." If one understands reality on truth as perceptions, then many complex social and individual acts are less disturbing. The "action" on "perceptions" is different than acting on "reality."

DR. MANUEL LIPSON
Senior Director, Massachusetts General Hospital
Pioneer in the study and practice of Physical Medicine and Rehabilitation at Harvard Medical School

252

SURRENDER

CCH POUNDER
Actor

SURVIVE

In *Waiting for Godot*, blind Pozzo, when asked where he is going, replies, "On." That's it.

STUDS TERKEL
Author
Winner of the 1985 Pulitzer Prize for *The Good War*

SVOBODA
СВОБОДА

FREEDOM LIBERTY

DR. ANDREI PIONTKOVSKY
Director, Center for Strategic Studies
Russian Federation

T. O.

GET A T. O. BABY!

Awesome Baby!

DICK VITALE
Basketball Commentator
ABC-TV and ESPN-TV

TASTE

I am in the business of nourishing. I encourage all to take the time to "taste" and enjoy life.

ANNE S. QUATRANO
Chef, Bacchanalia
Atlanta, Georgia

TENACITY

The world is made up of negative powers that demolish our dreams, leave people dejected and rejected. God wants us to grow in the struggle. It's been the only way to realize the dreams in my heart. God's grace has helped me to get up and start all over again—tenacity!

CAROL M. LAWRENCE
Actor, Singer

TENACITY

One has to stick to their convictions and never, never give up, no matter what the odds against are.

VINCENT J. NAIMOLI
Managing General Partner and Chief Executive Officer
Tampa Bay Devil Rays, Major League Baseball Team

TENACITY

If you know you are on the right track and others don't get your vision, tenacity will help your dream come true.

HENRY WINKLER
Actor, Producer, Writer, Director
"Fonzie" on *Happy Days*

THANK

THANK YOU.

"Thank you" is one of the most important things you can
say to a person. It is so simple to say although it is not used as
often as it should be.

DOUGLAS FAIRBANKS JR.
Actor, Producer, Writer

THANKFUL

Having started in a N.Y. City ghetto in the heart of the depression
(1928) I'm constantly reminded of how fortunate I've been in
being able to exploit God's athletic gifts in this wonderful country.

BOB COUSY
Former National Basketball Association Star
Boston Celtics
Member of the Basketball Hall of Fame
Model for the Logo of the National Basketball Association

THANKS

Give thanks for all of your undeserved blessings lest they be taken away.

TONY DUNBAR
Author

THANKS

I am so utterly thankful for everything in my life.

GAIL BUCKLEY
Author

THEM

IT'S THEM THAT DRAWS THE WATER LEAVES THE
BUCKET IN THE WELL.

My father's mother, born to poor hill people before the Civil
War, was the wisest person I've been privileged to know. She was
especially concerned to see those with the sense of duty to try
something, to act when action was called for, denigrated when
those actions were imperfect. I doubt that a day has gone by in
my adult life without some event, some remark, bringing this
admonition to my mind.

MILLER WILLIAMS
Author, Poet, Linguist, Translator
Inaugural Poet for the 1997 Inauguration of President Bill Clinton

THICK

NEVER GET INTO THE THICK OF THIN THINGS!

It will really help you in getting through life.

ROBERT BALLARD, PH.D.
Oceanographer, Found the *Titanic*

THINK

JULIE ANDREWS
Academy Award-Winning Actor

THIS

Couldn't begin to explain.

MICHAEL CUNNINGHAM
Author, Winner of the Pulitzer Prize for *The Hours*

THOUGHTFUL

It suggests both a dispassionate use of reason and consideration for others.

JUSTICE STEPHEN G. BREYER
United States Supreme Court Justice

THOUGHTFULNESS

Thoughtfulness is the miniaturization of the phrase
"Do unto others as you would have them do unto you."
For me, thoughtfulness is a step toward paradise.

WHOOPI GOLDBERG
Actor, Comedian
Academy Award for *Ghost*

TIME

TIME AND ABILITY

The two factors of success.

GENE FOWLER JR.
Film Director

TIME

A MAN MUST SHARE THE ACTION AND PASSION
OF HIS TIME, AT PERIL OF BEING JUDGED NOT
TO HAVE LIVED.

I have always felt Pat Holmes' admonition (contains) a few—of
many—words to live by.

PATRICK J. BUCHANAN
Politician, Author, and Television Commentator

TIME

TIME IS MONEY! DO IT NOW!

In today's world too much is lost by not accomplishing things immediately. Meetings and discussion often kill good ideas.

J. D. CARTER

TIME

"BY THE TIME, VERILY MAN IS IN LOSS, EXCEPT SUCH AS HAVE FAITH, AND DO RIGHTEOUS DEEDS, AND (JOIN TOGETHER) IN THE MUTUAL ENJOINING OF TRUTH, AND OF PATIENCE AND CONSTANCY."
—Sura Al-Asr, Holy Quran

This Sura refers to the testimony of time through the ages. All history shows that evil came to an evil end. But time is always in favour of those who have faith, live clean and pure lives, and know how to wait, in patience and constancy.

DR. TAYSEIR M. MANDOUR
Medical Doctor
Member, Interreligious Dialogue Commission, Egypt

TOLERANCE

Because "Peace."
Afterthought! As a theatrical clown, I would have chosen "flatulence" because it always gets a laugh.

OWEN BRYAN HULL
Broadway Actor
The longest-running actor in the same play: *The Fantastics*

TOLERANCE

Life is short and our Buddhist beliefs always remind us of transcendence of life. Because of this, one does not need to waste his time for non-important things, or collect too much unnecessary material things, or be angry with things that are not that important. We need to be tolerant to others.

SANJAASUREN OYUN
Member of Parliament
Leader of Citizens Will Party
Mongolia

TOLERANCE

I wish I had a better understanding of this word when I was growing up. The definition: The capacity to bear something unpleasant, painful or difficult—seems to apply to many situations in life.

PRISCILLA PRESLEY
Actor

TONGUE-TIED

There are so many words and such terrific things to say with them, but sometimes, for all of the world, I need to—I can't.

PAULA POUNDSTONE
Comedian, Television Personality

TOUCH

I sign everything with "touch." Most people sign with "love,"
"sincerely," or another word. I like to be an individual and not
follow everyone else's thoughts. I have a "touch" tattoo.
Touch is my way of saying "love" in a spiritual way.

MARY WILSON
Singer, An Original Member of The Supremes

TRADITION

I suppose the word that comes to my mind—and would come to
the mind of others if they were asked about me—is "Tradition."
For I have spent my scholarly life trying to understand the relation
between continuity and change in the way our past has understood
its past; I called my life work *The Christian Tradition*; I called my
Jefferson Lecture *The Vindication of Tradition*; and *Tradition* is
even the name of my sailboat.

JAROSLAV PELIKAN
Christian Church Historian, Author, Educator

TRADITION

Tradition is what unites us all, families and friends, countries and cultures. It is the crucible of a civilized society and fosters respect, manners and courtesy in youth, the elderly and every age in between. Respect for our own traditions teaches us tolerance for the traditions of others and thereby promotes understanding and ultimately peace.

DEBORAH RAFFIN
Actor, *7th Heaven*

TRANSFORMATION

It signifies the process of individuation, both in reference to the personal journey and the social struggle for justice and equity.

WALTER WINK
Author, Educator, Scholar in the Interpretation of the Bible

TRANSLATE

TRANSLATE IDEAS INTO EVENTS AND HELP PEOPLE.

A seven-word phrase that I would very much like to share
with you.

Senator Claiborne Pell
Former United States Senator from Rhode Island

TRUE

ONE WILL NOT FIND THE TRUE FIBER OF A MAN IN
TIMES OF PROSPERITY OR SUCCESS, BUT ONLY HIS
RESILIENCY IN TIMES OF TRIAL AND ADVERSITY.

I have had a lot of success in my life and I had always believed
that if I worked hard enough success was sure to follow. Sure I
encountered failure once in a while, but it was always an obstacle
I overcame quickly. However, it was not until later in my life
did I fully realize the larger meaning of adversity.

Sometimes it is only through pain and disappointment that
we can bring our life more into focus. I have realized failure in

human terms is meaningless. Failure is really about faith—whether that is faith in yourself, faith in your family, faith in a philosophy, or faith in a higher being. Faith is hard work. It is much easier just to throw in the towel. However, to quit is to lose hope, but to *persist* is to *prove* faith.

In life *attitude is everything*. When faced with adversity or failure, what counts is not so much the pain, but our attitude toward it. Suffering cannot be eliminated or changed, but our attitude toward it can be. Our resiliency proves our faith and in the end faith is what gets you through.

DALE BROWN
Retired Head Coach, Men's Basketball
Louisiana State University

TRUST

Every sustainable relationship, business or personal, whether formalized by contract, wedding vows, or a handshake—depends, in the final analysis, on trust.

ROBERT E. ALLEN
Chief Executive Officer
AT&T Corporation

TRUST

Trust—the centerpiece and the glue which molds one's character.

SENATOR BOB DOLE
Former United States Senator from Kansas
1996 Republican Nominee for President of the United States

TRUST

With trust as the foundation, a relationship can *grow* and *last* forever. Without trust, you never have a true relationship.

MIKE KRZYZEWSKI
Head Coach, Men's Basketball
Duke University

TRUST

Trust between people is the foundation of all successful and fulfilling endeavors. Without it there is no stability.

LORD MARSHALL OF KNIGHTSBRIDGE
Chairman, British Airways
United Kingdom

TRUST

Trust in the Lord and on His Love for each one of us is the key to holiness and to peace. Trust is the fruit of deep faith and from it comes love for God and for neighbor since when we rely on Him and on His promises, we become conscious of our belonging to His one human family.

THEODORE CARDINAL MCCARRICK
Roman Catholic Archbishop of Washington, D.C.

TRUTH

Life in our society would be remarkably better if we used it (truth) in our life more faithfully.

RICHARD E. GREENE
Regional Administrator for Region 6
Environmental Protection Agency
Former Mayor, Arlington, Texas

TRUTH

THE TRUTH IN TRUTHFULNESS!

I tried to do my scholarly work in this spirit.

HANS KUNG
Theologian, Author
President of the Global Ethic Foundation
Germany

TRUTH

TRUTH IS JUST ONE.

I believe that there is only one truth but many interpretations.

PETAR PISMESTROVIC
Editorial Cartoonist
Kleine Zietung
Austria

UNCONSCIONABLE

...it is wonderfully dire and dread—filled and has lost none of its moral force over time. It shouldn't be used casually but only when you need the perfect adjective to say "this just won't do!"

TED HOLMES
Television Journalist and Producer, CBS Television

UNDERSTAND

Trying to do so is at the root of everything good!

LEE C. BOLLINGER
President, Columbia University

URGENCY

Without a sense of urgency, things don't get done the way they should.

NORV TURNER
Coach in the National Football League, Miami Dolphins
Former Head Coach, Washington Redskins

US

NONE OF US IS AS SMART AS ALL OF US.

I believe it is true.

PHIL CONDIT
Chairman and Chief Executive Officer
The Boeing Company

VARIETY

I offer this word because that's what I said the last time I was asked for a word.

KURT SNIBBE
Editorial Cartoonist
ESPN

VIEWS

"EILU V'EILU DIVREI ELOHIM CHAIU" (Hebrew from the Talmud) "THESE, AND THESE ALSO, ARE THE WORDS OF THE LIVING GOD," REFERRING TO DIVERGENT AND EVEN CONFLICTING, VIEWS.

I think of it often, especially when I hear particularly dogmatic, or intolerant, statements. It reminds us to hold our views with humility, and of the need to afford tolerance and respect to conflicting views.

CONGRESSMAN JERROLD NADLER
Representive of the 8th Congressional District in New York

VISION

As mayor of the City of Louisville, Kentucky, I often seek the input of my fellow citizens on how they see our City and what vision they have for its future. I use the word *vision* perhaps 100 times during my daily rounds of conversations with fellow employees and other leaders because the word denotes creation and images that tend to be reflective of one's viewpoint.

DAVID ARMSTRONG
Former Mayor of Louisville, Kentucky

VISION

ECKHARD PFEIFFER
Former Chief Executive Officer of Compaq Computer Corporation
Chairman of Intershop

VISION

I am sending you a lexical gift, one word that I repeat so often and believe so vital for my being.

I believe it is critical for our generation to re-create a wholesome vision that connects us with our creator and gives us a meaningful relationship with His creation. We need to have a vision that helps us to be at peace with ourselves, with God and with our fellow beings. This vision should be able to give a sense of purpose beyond our earthly existence, and help us to sublimate our earthly drives.

I believe we are moving in that direction. There are many hurdles, moments of retrogression and backslides, but the direction towards a unified vision is evolving.

DR. SAYYID MUHAMMED SYEED
Secretary General
The Islamic Society of North America

VOICE

IF YOU ARE SILENT, YOU WILL REGRET YOUR SILENCE...
YOU ARE THE ULTIMATE, THE MOST POWERFUL, MOST
TRUSTWORTHY VOICE FOR THE PEOPLE YOU LOVE.

GERALDO RIVERA
Television Journalist, Fox News, *At Large with Geraldo Rivera*

WE

WE THE PEOPLE.

These are the first three words of the Preamble to the Constitution. The
Preamble is in some ways the most important part of the Constitution. It
sets out in a few brief eloquent words the founders' vision of what America
is all about. They're as real and as valid today as they were in 1787, and
I always find them inspiring. The first three words of the Preamble—
"We the People"—are especially important, because they mean that in
our country, the government is established to serve the people—meaning
all the people, including those who need our help the most, not just the
wealthy or the privileged or the powerful. In a sense, "We the People"
epitomizes the ideal of public service.

SENATOR EDWARD M. KENNEDY
United States Senator from Massachusetts

WEALTH

WEALTH IS CHILDREN.

A concept I learned during four years of living and working in Mali.

Sam Carlson
Executive Director, World Links

WELCOME

There are so many people excluded—groups against groups, whites against blacks. I think we should accept people for who and what they are regardless of race or creed or anything. We are all so different. I can understand why some groups would not be compatible and associate because they are so different, but they should be civil.

Clyde Connell
Artist, Sculptor

WELCOME

I use this word to try to "de-charge" emotions, events, etc. that
I judge as negative, in hopes that humor or detachment will give
me better perspective.

MEG RILEY
Director of the Department of Advocacy and Witness
Unitarian Universalist Association

WELL

WITHHOLD NO SACRIFICE
GRUDGE NO TOIL
SEEK NO SORDID GAIN
FEAR NO FOE
ALL WILL BE WELL
—Winston Churchill

GREGORY PECK
Actor

WHY?

It is the only question worth asking. And the question is more important than the answer. "Why?" is the source of wonder. "Why?" opens up the world.

JOHN DUFRESNE
Author
Teacher of Creative Writing at Florida International University

WHY?

Man's main quest in life.
All the answers known after life.

CORKY TRINIDAD
Cartoonist, *Honolulu Star Bulletin*

WILD

ISN'T THAT WILD!

As a mentalist or thought reader, I have spent my life presenting
on the stage and television some dramatic tests involving man's
capability, capacity, and mental skills. I have been told that in over
thirty-five years of television appearances when I have expressed
excitement and "wonder" at what a person does in response to
me, I have said the phrase, "Isn't that wild." In truth, I am so
unconscious of this spontaneous response that I hardly ever
remember saying it, though I suspect I must have thousands of
times. What I believe it therefore reflects is the total philosophical
wonderment I have for the human potential. The word philosophy
in its original definitions begins with the concept "to wonder"
and I think all of life is filled with such wonderment that it would
be tragic to ignore these miracles around us. God forbid that
I ever cease losing my sense of wonderment as I think it permeates
everything I ever do as a mentalist.

KRESKIN
Mentalist

WIND

Of spirit and flesh.

JAMES WHITEHEAD
Novelist, Poet

WINE

WINE IS IMAGINATION YOU CAN DRINK.

CRISTOBAL REINOSO
Editorial Cartoonist for *Clarin*
Argentina

WITHIN

JESUS SAID, "IF YOU BRING FORTH WHAT IS
WITHIN YOU, WHAT YOU BRING FORTH WILL
SAVE YOU. IF YOU DO NOT BRING FORTH WHAT
IS WITHIN YOU, WHAT YOU DO NOT BRING
FORTH WILL DESTROY YOU."
—Saying 70, *The Gospel According to Thomas*

When I first read this saying, which *The Gospel of Thomas*,
an ancient gospel recently discovered in Egypt, attributes to
"The living Jesus," I recognized initially that what it says is true.
All the time, I understood this saying on a psychological level.
Now I see it also as stating a spiritual axiom, based on the
conviction that each of us, being created "in the image of God,"
has internal spiritual resources that we need to explore.

ELAINE PAGELS
Author
Professor in the Department of Religion
Princeton University

WOMEN

WOMEN'S RIGHTS

It is in these two words that we can hold hope for humanity's healing and progress. Why? Because when women and girls have the opportunity to be educated and to work in a fair and free environment, they give back so much to their communities; when women live free of violence, they enjoy full, more productive lives; when women sit at the negotiating table, they bring new solutions to avoid war and military conflict. Most importantly, women activists, advocates, scholars and policy-makers who defend and promote human rights, improved the world for *everyone*.

These words have guided my work as President and CEO of the Global Fund for Women, the premier international foundation supporting creative and courageous women in 160 countries.

KAVITA N. RAMDAS
President and Chief Executive Officer, Global Fund for Women

WONDER

Often do I wonder
Gratefully because
Exhilarated by meeting
A scientific, artistic
Or spiritual joy.

But also wonder
Too often because
Dismayed by seeing
Lies and crimes inflict
So much misery.

DUDLEY R. HERSCHBACH
Nobel Laureate in Chemistry, 1986
Frank B. Baird Jr. Professor of Science
Harvard University

WORD

MY WORD IS MY BOND.

RED AUERBACH
Hall of Fame Former Coach of the
National Basketball Association's Boston Celtics

WORD

Our word is what creates our world. Keeping our word is what makes our world work.

DAVID FRIEDMAN
Musician

WORD

THE WORD IS ONLY AS GOOD AS THE PERSON
WHO STANDS BEHIND IT.

We can choose to accept the **word** of God and let it guide our daily life. We can choose **words** that can heal the hurt or inflict ill. Our **word** can be our bond of trust and love or it can be worthless utterances.

What we say in **words** can be mankind's epitaph in history or shame for all time. Choose your **words** from the heart and not from the lips. The quietest whisper of understanding often carries thunderous messages to the world.

ROBERT "BOB" HEFT
Designer of the Current National Flag
of the United States of America

WORK

HARD WORK OVERCOMES ADVERSITY.

Too much is made of why things cannot be done. I've observed countless numbers of young men, like Steve Kerr, who accomplished great things despite adversity.

LUTE OLSON
Head Coach, Men's Basketball, University of Arizona
1997 NCAA Champions

WRITING

THE BEST WRITING IS RE-WRITING.

In anything you create, in my case words and music, don't quit too soon. Even if you think you are finished, keep working on it, and you are usually able to improve it.

JAY LIVINGSTON
Composer, Lyricist

YEARNING

Fiction is the art form of human yearning.

ROBERT OLEN BUTLER
Author
Winner of a 1993 Pulitzer Prize for *A Good Scent from a Strange Mountain*
Professor, Florida State University

YES

It is an affirmation; a gift of permission to think positively and take action. "Yes" is a rejection of negativity. It is the word that allows all things to be positive in life.

ANN RICHARDS
Former Governor of Texas

YES

Because that word has preceded my most memorable and enjoyable encounters.

WYNTON MARSALIS
Trumpeter, Multiple Grammy Winner

YES

I had a high school football coach who taught me at a very young age that I could do things no one, including myself, believed I could. His name was Homer Beatty. Later I played for Vince Lombardi who taught and believed the same thing. What they taught and believed, besides football, was commitment, dedication, hard work and the awareness of that inner voice that says, "Yes I can."

FRANK GIFFORD
Hall of Fame National Football League Player
Television Sportscaster

YOU

IF YOU WANT SOMETHING DONE PROPERLY,
DO IT YOURSELF.

ROSAMUNDE PILCHER
Author

YOU

If you want readers to respond, the most important topic, the one they care about most, is themselves. In other words, "you."

ROBERT BLY
Poet, Author

EPILOGUE

WHAT'S YOUR WORD?

The last gripping scenes in the Broadway musical *Man of La Mancha* tug at emotions and challenge a singular reliance on reason. Self-serving enemies, posing as compassionate friends, have robbed the visionary character Don Quixote of his life-giving dream, deriding both the dream and the man as fanciful at best and crazy at worst. The once proud knight lies corpse-like on a couch; his dream is dead and he is dying. Enter Quixote's loyal sidekick Sancho and the love of his life, a woman of the streets named "Aldonza" whom Quioxte called "Dolcinea." Grateful for the positive changes in her life that Quixote's words and vision have wrought in her life, Aldonza feels her heart breaking; her grand hero can neither recognize nor remember her. Obviously she was a part of the dream now gone. But, Aldonza will not give up easily; she refuses to allow the "Knight of the Woeful Countenance" to be robbed of that which gave life to him and to her. Strenuously seeking to touch the Knight's consciousness and stir his memory, Aldonza repeats some of the most memorable words given to her by Quixote. It works; the words work! A sudden twitch signals life in the man's apparently lifeless body.

A twinkle cracks the glaze that had covered his eyes. Quixote stirs, then moves and stretches; he is coming to life again. The fallen Knight tries to remember, desperately reaching into the past in hopes of continuing his noble mission in the future. "The words," Don Quixote says to Aldonza with soulful passion, "Tell me the words." I understand the intensity of that plea and the incredible passion with which Quixote articulates it. Words stir imagination, inform memory, and fire energy. Words give life as well as make possible an identification of life and direction for life. Most importantly, words connect reality and dreams.

The kind of urgency that laced Quixote's pleading for words from Aldonza has fueled my requests for words from other people. I know the promise resident in an individual's positive response to the question "Will you give me a word?"—the inestimable value of a persons' gift of a word. With the coming of words arrive insight and understanding, identification and inspiration, hopes and dreams, expectations and vision.

"The words, tell me the words!"

WORDS AND WORK

As you have perused the word gifts in this little book, you may have noticed no obvious link between a particular word and the profession of its contributor. However, in some instances, a connection between a contributor's word and that contributor's work is too obvious to miss. Business leaders and religious leaders, most noticeably, tended to share words integrally related to their respective corporate lives and spiritual traditions. Frequently, persons from these professions even used my request to contribute to this book as an opportunity to promote their particular business, to sell their profession, or to commend to others an important dimension of their personal faith. That is not surprising. The words most vibrant with life emerge from the center of our lives nurtured by the commitments that give the most meaning to our lives.

A WORD IN TIME

Whether or not a word in time is like the "stitch" in the old adage—"a stitch in time saves nine"—I do not know. The math of words escapes me. I do know, however, that an integral relationship exists between words and the time in which they are written or spoken, mulled over alone or shared with others.

One contributor to this project attached a note to her word gift, explaining that she was forwarding to me her word for the moment, implying that another moment, a different time, well could inspire another word from her. To be sure, their setting in time, the very specific historical context within which they were born, enhanced mightily the words in this volume offered by two former presidents of the United States. In each instance the calming, comforting words of these two leaders echoed in sharp contrast to the harsh reverberations of strident sounds so prevalent during the particular historical period of struggle in which their words had been conceived. Several of the word gifts that arrived during the national debate over United States military action in Iraq reflected deep-seated concerns related to peace. Ambassador Jean Kennedy Smith's word, though tiny in size, opens a large vista onto a collage of images—some happy and some as sad as they are tragic—drawn from the well-publicized history of her family. How moving the word; how different things could have been!

A WORD ABOVE TIME

While some words are products of a particular time, other words transcend time—words for all seasons. Love is such a word; the word most popular among contributors to this collection of words. Clear from the varied explanations that accompanied gifts of the word "love," though, is a realization that people's preference for the word "love" had less to do with sentimentality or social popularity than with a recognition of the necessity of relationships built on the phenomenon that the word "love" names.

Contributors to this volume also displayed a strong affinity for naming deity. No doubt you noted the number of people who gave me the word "God." Equally interesting, but not surprising, contributors recognized the importance of a sense of responsibility in life and applauded the virtue of integrity. How good! How encouraging. Such words signal an interest in respect, reverence, trustworthiness, and honesty—bricks essential to building a civil, compassionate, and just society.

WORDS, WORDS, WORDS

Well, there you have it—my collection of words, 351 different words, (actually more words than that if all the words in all of the favored phrases are counted) from 506 different individuals. Each of these words reveals an important memory, studied thought, a cherished relationship, professional commitment, an ordered priority, a sense of humor, commended values, religious conviction, profound hope and/or the personal interest of its giver. What great gifts words make—insightful, inspirational, beautiful, educational gifts.

I cannot get enough of them. Every word given to me is endowed with irreplaceable value and a source of continuing appreciation.

Now, one more matter remains, one more word to be spoken or written—a word from you. I now turn to you the readers with the question that I have posed to hundreds of would-be contributors to this volume. What is your word?

Please reflect on my question. Talk about it with family, friends, and colleagues if you will. I encourage you to answer my inquiry; answer it in a manner that brings you satisfaction. Once you know "your word," you may want to keep it to yourself, massage it with your mind, feel it with your emotions, look at it, seek to understand it, and learn from it. Eventually, though, I hope you will heed my commendation of a grand adventure in thoughtful generosity. I urge you to share your word with a person or with persons who will gratefully receive it for what it is—a precious gift—and maybe respond by sharing their word. All involved will benefit from that exchange of gifts. I give you my word.

IN OTHER WORDS

Virtually everybody I know well contributed to this book in one way or another. Some suggested potential contributors, others agreed to share my request for a word with someone to whom they had access, and still others did both. This collection of words is stronger and richer as a result of the helpfulness of these people who number far too many to be named here individually.

A few persons, however, invested in this word project with a level of generosity and interest without which its completion would be in question. The names of several of these individuals appear in the book already—Will Campbell, Judith Light, Heber Jentzsch and Bob Dilenschneider—because they contributed words of their own as well as aided my search for words from others. Several individuals offered substantive assistance apart from any thoughts about inclusion in this volume, though frequently and playfully speculating aloud about what word they would choose were I to ask them to give me a word. Since, in the course of regular interactions with these people, I have become aware of the words that would have been their respective gifts—I have asked each of them to give me a word—I place each of their words alongside their names with bountiful thanks for all of their contributions to this book and to my life.

Ron Stewart (**TOMORROW**) suggested directories to consult and demonstrated a level of interest in this project that proved inspirational. Herb Hamsher (**AUTHENTICITY**), Joan Avagliano (**PATIENCE**), Freida Brian (**DETERMINATION**), and Jim Weighardt (**PASSION**) made possible my contact with numerous persons whom I otherwise would not have been able to reach. I am most grateful.

I appreciate my colleagues in The Interfaith Alliance and The Interfaith Alliance Foundation across the years, especially the Vice President, Suzie Armstrong (**HOME**), who endured my endless talk about this project and kindly repressed questions about how and why a collection of words could be so important to me.Special recognition and expressions of appreciation go to my professional assistant Maggy Alexander (**PEACE**) who, in the process of offering help related to this book, discovered for herself the excitement of opening a piece of mail that contains the gift of a word, and to my very good personal friend Patti Pate (**PASSION**), a university instructor in English, who drafted several versions of my work and helped me to get it in final form, caring about the words as well as processing them. My editor,

Mary Aarons (**BONA FIDE**), has been a constant source of encouragement and helpful guidance.

From my immediate family, no one specific act of assistance, though many such acts occurred, was more important than their sustained understanding (or loyalty-based attempts at understanding) of my devotion to this project and their encouragement for me to pursue it to completion (though occasionally gently observing that they hoped it did not take forever). Gratitude intermingles with love as I recognize the multidimensional support of my wife, Judy (**I DO**), and the unfailing affirmation that comes from our daughter-in-law, Amanda (**DEDICATION**), our sons James (**LAUGH**) and John Paul (**TEAM**), and our grandson, Reynolds, who, in an emphatic guttural tone uncharacteristic for a two-year-old, blesses me with the indescribably emotional and unfathomably meaningful gift of his word for me—"PapPaaw!"